RELIGIOUS
RITE & CEREMONY
IN MILTON'S POETRY

**A UNIVERSITY OF
KENTUCKY STUDY**

Αʼμαθεῖ γεγράφθαι χειρὶ τήνδε μὲν εἰκόνα
Φαίης τάχ᾽ ἄν, πρὸς εἶδος αὐτοφυὲς βλέπων·
Τὸν δ᾽ ἐκτυπωτὸν ὂκ ἐπιγνόντες φίλοι
Γελᾶτε φαύλȣ δυσμίμημα ζωγράφȣ.

RELIGIOUS
RITE & CEREMONY
IN MILTON'S POETRY

by Thomas B. Stroup

UNIVERSITY OF KENTUCKY PRESS
Lexington, 1968

*For those students who in the classroom
have shared with me
the Miltonic rite*
TE DEUM LAUDAMUS

The present study has grown out of my frequent reading of Milton, not as Puritan or other partisan, but rather as *vates*, poet-prophet, for so he considered his calling. As such, he must also perform the priestly office, not to be dissociated from the other two, by making the proper oblation and petitions, as intermediary. In doing so, he required recognizable formularies, ritual, or ceremony suggested or given, or liturgical references to make clear his office and his meaning. The preacher was prophet; he functioned also as presbyter. If Isaiah is to speak as God's prophet, he must have God's ordination, the touch of the coal to his lips from off the sacred altar; so also must the poet if he is to "prevent" the Magi with his ecstatic hymn of praise and thanksgiving. If the priest-prophet is to present his great argument, he must call upon the Creator Spirit to enlighten him as one ordained to justify God's ways. By such means, by rituals and ceremonies and echoes from liturgy, Milton confirms his conception of the office and vocation of the poet, and by such he enriches the meaning of his work. Recognition aids understanding; and the singularity of their form and use—for ofte they are not easily recognizable nor their function readi' perceived—reveals also a notable characteristic of Miltor art which I hope I make explicit.

ACKNOWLEDGMENTS

To the University of Kentucky I render humble and hearty thanks for two summer research fellowships, one held in 1965 and another in 1966, which helped me to complete this work. It is a special pleasure—and my bounden duty and service—to acknowledge and confess my manifold debts and obligations to Professor Mary Ellen Rickey and to Professor Douglas Bush. Their suggestions have added substance to this work, and their reading of the manuscript has saved me from error. To my wife, who of her great kindness has heard my bitter complaints and of her great industry has patiently typed the manuscript, I am most grateful. That I may count upon her ever present help in the later times when errors may be found or judgments questioned assures me of a blessed future obligation.

CONTENTS

INTRODUCTION

IN HIS now-famous lecture upon Milton, T. S. Eliot in 1947 advised contemporary poets to study Milton "as, outside the theatre, the greatest master in our language of freedom within form."[1] Although the words "freedom within form" seem in this context to be restricted to technical matters of verse and verse forms and the advice to poets, the "freedom" might have been equally well extended to materials and doctrines, and the advice to critics and commentators. For with Milton, form was always handmaiden to substance. Critic of custom of any kind and advocate of the new liberties of his age as he understood them in both his verse and prose, he could not in good countenance have expressed his criticism or his advocacy by adhering strictly to generic forms or following closely the rules of prosody. Yet for him the bolder outlines, the larger aspects, the basic patterns of established forms and genres must not go unregarded. "Each of his important poems," Professor Barker writes, ". . . depends very largely on a recognition of likeness as the basis for expressive variation."[2] No necessary adjunct or true ornament to verse, rime may be a hindrance and constraint to expression; but basic meter should not go lame, and the ancient and recognized genres, reformed and adapted, may well serve the new liberties of the age. A Greek pastoral elegy, with the form only a little modified, will furnish a melodious tear for a young English cleric, whose passing will be mourned by such oddly assorted voices as Apollo's, the River Cam's, Triton's, and St. Peter's—the report of a ritual adapted to say "*Pax vobiscum.*" A Greek tragedy with choruses in *apolelymenon* echoing the Psalms presents the fall of an heroic Hebrew to provide an heroic example of trust in God's providence. Or a classical epic, deviating in structure from Renaissance theory and somewhat modified in form by the influence of the epics of Dante, Spenser, and others, sets forth the most ancient story of man's first disobedience and the Fall not less but more heroic than that of Homer, Virgil, or Ariosto, and much concerned with the origin of creatures and customs in its attempt to justify God's ways to men. And so one might continue to illustrate variously.

But my concern here is with only one aspect of the subject. Perhaps it would be more nearly correct, as this study turns out, to speak of it as form within freedom, rather than the other way round. It has to do with one of the materials out of which men make poetry, or if we like, two materials: rites and ceremonies.

Now, as all readers know, Milton said disrespectful things about ritual and ceremony, especially about liturgies and rites; generally, he discredited them—at least those which had to do with religion.[3] Yet he made use of them in his poetry. When the occasion called for it, a formalized and ceremonious action would take place, frequently so unobtrusively and so submerged as scarcely to be recognized as belonging to any classifiable ritual. In some cases it is doubtful that the poet himself recognized such actions for what they were; in others he might defend them as spontaneous expressions later to become ritualized through repetition. And yet they were formalized acts and their occasions were recurring ones, such as morning prayers or grace before meat or a marriage ceremony, or even a formal greeting such as "Hail." The terms—rites and ceremonies—are interchangeable. Each of these materials is lifted by human emotion out of routine human action, set aside and given a familiar form, dramatized as it were. In actual social intercourse, if sincerely performed, such formalized actions serve to sharpen awareness and heighten experience. Intensified, they become basic for the poet, especially the narrative poet and the dramatic poet. Willy nilly, he cannot do without them. In this study I intend to examine in primarily chronological order Milton's use of such materials in his poetry. I will concentrate, in particular, upon representative examples of recognized religious rituals and ceremonies, those expressed completely, those given in part, and those merely suggested or referred to. By so doing I hope I may increase somewhat our understanding of his poetry and somewhat the nature of his art.

That Milton was especially well acquainted with religious ritual, liturgy, and ceremony is not to be questioned. He was baptized in Allhallows Church in Breadstreet and as a boy attended its services faithfully, we can be sure, along with his family. It seems probable that his father, a well-recognized musician and composer, was interested in the music sung at Allhallows; even probable that some of his father's own compositions from Ravenscroft's compendium of church music and some from Leighton's *Teares and Lamentations* were sung there. Among his compositions in Myriell's *Tristitiae Remedivm* is a setting of an old Latin hymn as a motet: with its *Gloria Patri* it would serve well the place of a canticle for Evensong.[4] At St. Paul's School the poet as a boy attended daily prayers, very probably the service of Morning Prayer as set forth in the Elizabethan version of the Book of Common Prayer. We know that he was required to attend morning and evening prayers throughout his seven years at Christ's College. As ritual he knew, then, the great canticles of the Church—the *Venite*, the *Benedicite, omnia opera Domini*, the *Te Deum*, the *Benedictus*, the *Magnificat*, the *Nunc dimittis*—as well as the Confessions, the Creeds, and all the prayers of Matins, Evensong, and the Communion. Countless repetitions of these carved their words upon his memory; and although he knew their Biblical sources, he knew them first and remembered them best as functioning, organic manifestations of the covenant of grace from the Book of Common Prayer, from Sternhold and Hopkins, from Ravenscroft's *Whole Book of Psalms*, and such other paraphrases as the Bay Psalm Book, William Barton's, George Sandys', Zachary Boyd's, and others,[5] just possibly some from John Knox's Book of Common Order, and from primers and other collections of prayers and ritual.

Significantly Milton's era was a time of liturgy making. Following the practices of the compilers before him, Cranmer had built his Prayer Book out of earlier liturgies, adapting what he found suitable to his needs and fusing newer parts from the Scriptures. John Knox built his rites upon earlier ones and in the same way. Bishop Lancelot Andrewes, whom Milton admired, wrote his liturgies; his rite for the consecration of a church is still used. Under Archbishop Laud's direction the rejected Scottish Prayer Book was drawn up. Jeremy Taylor was an industrious compiler of liturgies. His Communion Service was designed to please a broad church. Each one of Donne's *Devotions upon Emergent Occasions* is in its three parts a liturgy. Henry Lawes, Milton's associate, wrote liturgical music. And there were numerous others. It would be surprising if Milton, quite aware of the practices, did not bend them to his service. Out of a fusion of Scriptural passages and familiar prayers and liturgy, he might, as his predecessors and contemporaries did, suggest rites and ceremonies appropriate to his poetry.

However much in later life he may have objected to

4

ritual or liturgy, he could never escape their impact from the days of his youth. Their well-remembered words often echo in his verses as cues to their occasions and suggest to wary readers the motifs of their forms deep within the poem. Likewise the watchful may recognize a ceremonial or emergent rite in the form and substance of the poem as a whole.

1

THE MINOR POEMS

$\mathcal{M}$ILTON'S shorter poems show numerous instances of liturgical influence. In the Nativity Ode, for example, the twofold expression of sacred rite is apparent. The gift of the hymn to the heaven-born child comes from one whose lips have been touched with sacred fire from off Isaiah's altar.[1] He speaks as priest and prophet, and his gift of words becomes a sacred ceremony transcending time; he joins his voice to the angel choir to sing with them the most joyous of all canticles, the *Gloria in excelsis*. Stanzas IX through XIV, most expressive of the theme of the poem, are an ecstatic celebration of "Glory be to God on high, and on earth peace, good will towards men." Within his gift of praise and thanksgiving—and central to it—is the remembered, though unrecited, portion of liturgy which, as chanted in church, is an eleboration of the words of the Herald Angels. It is not enough to repeat the words of the angels or the Church's elaboration of them as they appeared at the end of the Communion Service of Elizabeth's Book of Common Prayer; the true celebrant must add his own words to those of the angels. Generally, Milton's practice is not unlike the method of the compilers of liturgies; underneath lies the form and the cue to its presence, but the new words refresh its meaning.

An example is *At a Solemn Music*. The concert of religious music is conceived of as a religious ceremony of praise. The speaker calls upon voice and verse to join with instruments to elevate man's "fantasy" so that he may realize his service as one with the eternal rites performed by the saints before the throne of God. The imagery is taken from the vision of Ezekiel as it becomes fused with that of Revelation (xiv, 2-4), in which just spirits sing a new song as they move about the throne. Their ritual anticipates that in *Paradise Lost*, VII, 594-607, with its canticle. The petition at the end of the poem calls for a return to the heavenly harmony lost at the Fall. The poet not only describes the heavenly ritual but also wishes and hopes that his may become a part of that solemn service. He is again a compiler of liturgy.

Since *The Passion* is incomplete, we cannot be sure of its ceremonial or ritualistic value, but assuredly the poet assumes the priestly character as he approaches the subject "above the years he had,"[2] and it is likely he intended such ritualistic connections as appear in the Nativity Ode, perhaps even developing them from the Gospel for Good Friday, John xviii and xix, or, better, Psalm xxii as set aside for the day.[3]

On the Circumcision, if not a ritual itself, celebrates a primary Jewish rite which was transformed into the Christian sacrament of Baptism and, according to St. Paul, into the

7

Eucharist as well. Milton was well aware of this. Addressed to those same flaming powers with whom he sang at the Nativity, it calls for a very different canticle from what was sung on that occasion, one expressing sorrow, not only for the pain involved in the rite, but also in anticipation of the Passion later to come which would completely fulfill the Covenant. This rite celebrates and seals in itself the first obedience, and this seal of obedience is precisely the theological interpretation of the place of the Circumcision in the Church calendar. The collect for the day in the Prayer Book stresses the obedience of the Son and its meaning: "Almightie God, which madest thy blessed sonne to bee Circumcised, and obedient to the lawe for man, graunt vs the true Circumcision of the spirit, that our hartes . . . may in all thynges obey they blessed will." The lessons for the day concern the covenant made with Abraham in the Old Testament and its interpretation by St. Paul in the New. For Milton a sacrament is the affirmation of a covenant with God.[4] If we remember that the Christian equivalent of Circumcision is Baptism, wherein promises are made to obey the Ten Commandments, the Mosaic Covenant, we may the better appreciate the implications of the poem. We may find in its anticipation of the Passion of the cross an adumbration of the New Covenant to be sealed by the symbol of the new sacraments.

Taken as a whole *Comus* can hardly be said to constitute a single, sustained ritual, but within its parts are two well defined rites. In fact, the two oppose each other, the one used to complicate the plot, the other to resolve it; the one evil, the other good. In his first appearance Comus, calling upon his beastly followers, says, "Come let us our rites begin,/ 'Tis only daylight that makes sin," whereupon he hails "Dark veil'd *Cottyto*," a mysterious dame who rides with Hecate, and calls upon her to befriend him and his train, her priests. Following this invocation Comus and his rout perform their dance, their rites, which is broken off as the Lady, their sacrifice, appears. A second part of Comus' rites

8

is performed offstage, for the next scene in which he appears is a stately palace. Here through magic he has produced a banquet and enchanted the Lady, though he has failed to seduce her. Later her brothers rush in to break the spell and save their sister, but they succeed only in driving off the enchanter and his rout. They fail to capture his wand, by which "revers't / And backward matters of dissevering power" they could have freed the Lady from her chair. This situation makes necessary counter magic, or counter ritual. An invocation is sung, "Sabrina fair," calling the water spirit from her stream to free the Lady. The song is followed by a long incantation worded according to proper formulary— either pagan or Christian. It begins

> Listen and appear to us
> In name of great *Oceanus*,
> By the earth-shaking *Neptune's* mace
> And *Thetys'* grave majestic pace,
> By hoary *Nereus'* wrinkled look
> And the *Carpathian* wizard's hook, (ll. 867-72)

and continues through twelve more lines to summon the nymph in the names of six more sea deities as well as the Sirens and all the other water nymphs. Sabrina then rises, attended by her nymphs, and, having sung the lovely "By the rushy-fringed bank", performs her interesting rite. It consists really in stage directions: Sabrina tells her audience what she does, and that is all:

> Brightest Lady look on me,
> Thus I sprinkle on thy breast
> Drops that from my fountain pure
> I have kept of precious cure,
> Thrice upon thy finger's tip,
> Thrice upon thy rubied lip;
> Next this marble venom'd seat
> Smear'd with gums of glutinous heat
> I touch with chaste palms moist and cold.
> Now the spell hath lost its hold;
> And I must haste ere morning hour
> To wait in Amphitrite's bow'r. (ll. 910-21)

9

The rite is described and acted; the release is secured by what is done, not what is said.

As the Asperges performed by the Priest in Act I of Fletcher's *Faithful Shepherdess* (to which Milton was probably indebted) cleanses the assembled shepherds, so this ceremony removes from the Lady all taint of association with evil and the fascination with it which holds her in the chair.[5] But whereas Fletcher's is an obvious and outright Asperges in which the Priest purges by words as well as water, Milton's is modified in form and partially disguised by being intermingled with another rite or two. The particularized and individualized sprinkling of the breast, fingers, and lips may, for example, suggest the ritual of purifying by the sign of the cross one's forehead, lips, and breast before the reading of the Gospel at the Mass; or it may even suggest the individual's purification by the use of holy water as he enters the church. The form is recognizable, but freedom within form. It is not just a piece of magic as on the surface it would seem, but is endowed with the values of at least one Christian rite based upon the moving words of Psalm li, the *Miserere mei, Deus*, the noblest of the Penitential Psalms. The meaning and value of *Comus* are further enhanced once we recognize that the action depends entirely upon the two double rites.[6] The first provides the epitasis, the second the denouement of the plot.

Everyone who approaches *Lycidas* is told that it is a pastoral elegy and that it conforms to certain conventions such as the lament in which destiny is questioned, the procession of mourners who pass by the bier, the refrain, and the consolation. A ritual is set up, as before me others have noted,[7] and *Lycidas* becomes a ritualistic poem. What perhaps has not been observed so often is how Milton adapts the classical conventions to suggest a Christian memorial service for the dead or a burial rite.[8] The schema enables us to recognize in the poem the sermon-meditation, the interior ritual, and the memorial.

For it is not until the reader comes to the stanza of

ottava rima at the end that he realizes the poem has a dramatic framework: what has been said is a report of what the "uncouth swain" one day meditated among his pastures and trees. Up until this point the reader or hearer presumes he is hearing or overhearing a monody coming unpremeditated from the lips of its creator; now he knows differently. What seemed extempore has suddenly become studied and worthy of repetition. Whether or not the speaker is the "uncouth swain" dramatizing himself, he has dramatically removed his reader or hearer one step further away in tense and in person from the "fiction" and has made the meditation a remembered thing, a memorial service fitting for those who shall come after Lycidas to wander in that perilous flood.

Within the monody proper is a complex of meditation-sermon and ritual. To try to separate the two would be to divide substance from form: better they should be treated together. At the outset the shepherd meditates, not only the bitter constraint and sad occasion, but the very theme or text of the sermon—the apparent waste of both constraint and occasion. The meditation and the invocation of the Muses lead to a statement of the appropriate ritual, a *pax vobiscum*, a *requiescat* for his friend:

> Hence with denial vain, and coy excuse,
> So may some gentle Muse
> With lucky words favor my destin'd Urn,
> And as he passes turn,
> And bid fair peace be to my sable shroud. (ll. 18-22)

He proposes to do for his friend what he hopes someone may do for him when his time comes. His Muse begins with a loudly swept string to give some account of the lives of the two together, the sort of biographical material found in the Christian funeral oration and sermon.[9] This is interrupted by a lament and the meditation upon the loss. The meditation leads to the rebellious questioning of the value of scorning delights and living laborious days, especially if the blind Fury comes early to slit the thin-spun life. Both the question and the reply are couched in words such as preachers use: one should learn early that fame is no plant that grows on mortal soil. Following this outburst, and with the same intense fancy which brought Phoebus upon the scene, comes the rite within the ritual: the imagined procession of mourners past the imagined bier, a ceremony as Christian as it was pagan. Then the last of the mourners, himself among the first of Christian preachers, delivers his Reformation sermon against the corrupt clergy. (Among others, it reminds one of Colet's famous sermon before the Convocation for the Extirpation of Heresy at St. Paul's in 1512.) His dread voice is the voice of the preacher, no epic strain. The meditative pastoral-like flower passage suggests the garlands used to bedeck the bier in the ritual, except again the bier is a false surmise: the body of the shepherd is washed far away on the ocean floor. The imagined ceremony is set over against the stern reality of the last question posed in the funeral sermon, as well as the bitter loss expressed, a loss not made the less by Phoebus' reminder that fame is reserved for heaven. The answer comes in the consolation.

And it comes with Biblical and liturgical echoes. As Lycidas has sunk beneath the watery floor, so sank the day-star—not merely the sun, but the Son, for in Scripture He was called the Day-Star. And in Scripture (Luke i:68 ff.), as it was transferred into the liturgy and called the *Benedictus*, He was called "the day-spring from on high." As the Day-Star rose, "the bright and morning star," to "flame in the forehead of the morning sky," so Lycidas has risen. The poet is at some pains, I believe, to suggest the consolation of the *Benedictus* and to cue the reader to Luke's joyous promise that this Day-Spring from on high who has visited us has come "To geue light to them that sitte in darchnes, and in the shadow of death: and to guyde our feete into the waye of peace." Both in imagery and import the consolation suggests several passages from the burial services in the several versions of the Book of Common Prayer, but chiefly perhaps the Collect for the office in the first Prayer Book of

Edward VI, wherein it is asked that "bothe we and oure brother departed . . . may with all thyne elect Saynctes, obteine eternall joye . . . by the meanes of our aduocate Jesus Christ:" that is, "Through the dear might of him that walk'd the waves."

But of course the consolation in *Lycidas* also reminds us of the *consolatio* of the funeral or memorial sermons, itself a formulary. For example, at the end of his sermon at the funeral of Bishop Andrewes, John Buckeridge, Bishop of Ely, remarks that the saintly Andrewes had died, as he had lived, "in the Lord," and that such as he " 'From henceforth, saith the Spirit, they rest from their labours;' all tears are wiped from their eyes, and all sighs from their hearts."[10] It should be remembered that Milton's *Elegia Tertia* was written "On the Death of the Bishop of Winchester," Lancelot Andrewes, and that in this poem the speaker recounts a dream vision in which he sees the gentle bishop received by the heavenly hosts and hears a voice saying, "Nate, veni, et patrii felix cape gaudia regni; / Semper ab hinc duro, nate, labore vaca." (Come, my son, and enter joyfully into the pleasures of your father's kingdom; here rest forever from your labor.) Possibly Milton heard the sermon and thought of the *consolatio* as he wrote; more likely he is remembering the passage as a formulary, knowing, of course, its source in Scripture. Assuredly, he is not paraphrasing the words from the Revelation of St. John directly as if they had never before been used in a consolation. Rather, when he writes "And wipe the tears for ever from his eyes," he expects the reader to associate the line immediately with rite and formulary, with high ceremony and priestly idiom.

He might equally well expect the reader to associate with ritual the stanza of ottava rima at the end. The memorial sermon and the office of the Burial of the Dead alike furnish consolation for the living. The example set by him who is now entertained by all the saints, whether Bishop Andrewes or Edward King called Lycidas, sustains those left alive in the tasks set for their tomorrows. The stanza then serves the

13

purpose of the *"Ite"* at the end of the Mass or one of the many benedictions and dismissals which come at the close of any Christian rite or service. Cleansed by the experience now and reassured of God's providence, the participant is ready to go forth and, as a true, warfaring Christian, carry out God's purposes. He faces about and carries on. The stanza quite properly provides this look toward the future. It has the moving effect of the last acts of the military burial ceremony, which comes to its close, not with Taps nor yet with the firing of the salute, but rather with the ruffle of drums, the "about face," and the quickstep. The symbolism is apparent. Ritual merges with nonritual, the finite with the infinite, time with the timeless. Milton has achieved the ultimate purpose of ritual and has written his liturgy—without loss of spontaneity.[11]

2

PARADISE LOST

$\mathcal{M}$ILTON'S adaptations and modifications of literary forms and genres in *Paradise Lost* are so varied and so well done that one may not at first recognize them as such. The poem is first and obviously a classical epic, though much modified; the basic form and materials are here, but greatly enriched, and extended far beyond the limits of such an epic as Virgil wrote. In his emulation of precedent, as Coleridge observed, Milton expanded and improved it.[1] Among other kinds, the poem is, though not so obviously, also a Christian religious epic, a Biblical commentary, a homily, and, if we take into account the origin of its substance and its first forms in mystery and morality play, a sort of epic drama. Into the whole the poet incorporates numerous lesser genres, among them orations, sermons, anthems, canticles, prayers, and other ritualistic, liturgical, and ceremonial bits and fragments. Apparently the ritualistic genres and materials among these adaptations and modifications, their place and value in the poem in whole or in part, have gone pretty much unregarded—both by Coleridge and by subsequent critics as well.

With their part as a force shaping the poem as a whole I am briefly concerned. First, conceived as drama on the order of mystery-morality play, the poem retains in its larger aspects some of the liturgical qualities of its antecedents. The angelic choruses sung in Books III, VI, VII, and X resemble in kind and in function the choruses of the angels in the York Cycle, or their singing the *Gloria in excelsis* in the *Second Shepherds' Play*. Just as the angelic choruses come at moments of high intensity and change in the plays (as Nan Cooke Carpenter has pointed out),[2] so they come in *Paradise Lost* and just so came the great canticles in the liturgies of the church, some of them derived from the songs of angels as recorded in Scripture. From Scripture to liturgy to plays to poem, is a long descent. Yet Milton was aware of it, and with him the practice comes full circle, and he fully recognized the Scriptural origins of liturgy and Christian rites. Since *Paradise Lost* deals so much with the beginning of things, as given in Scripture, its account often merely suggests the origins of liturgies, rites, and ceremonials of many kinds and presents their emergence in the simplest form, unsullied and uncluttered by time. The high pronouncements of the Father and the Son and the canticles sung by the angels before the golden altar and the celestial throne, the incense burning the while, suggest nothing less than the perpetual service of praise and thanksgiving as described in the Apocalypse. Individually, they suggest various parts of liturgy. These will be my later concern.

Just now we must speculate, for what it may be worth,

upon the general pattern of liturgy as a shaping force in *Paradise Lost*, whether or not the poet deliberately followed it. Very generally the basic parts of liturgy, at least the liturgies Milton was most familiar with, were these and followed with little deviation this order: a call to prayer, repentance and confession, absolution, instruction and praise, intercessions, thanksgiving, and benediction. The Christian comes into the church soiled by sin and in despair, but with a broken and a contrite heart he confesses his sin and achieves forgiveness, expressed in the absolution. He then is instructed through the reading of the two lessons (or in the Lord's Supper, in the reading of the Epistle and Gospel), interspersing the reading with praise and thanksgiving in the form of canticles. Now cleansed and properly instructed, he is able to make his intercessions and petitions to God and to be strengthened by these and, if the service is the Lord's Supper, by the communion. Blessed, he may now go forth thankfully to face the world again.[3] The pattern, with many variations, of course, may easily be recognized in the morality plays, among them Milton's own plan for *Adam Unparadised*. It is recognized less easily in some of the secular plays of the Elizabethan period. Notably, it becomes apparent in the *Faerie Queene*, especially in the latter cantos of Book I and Book II. The later and more secular writers must in their fictions show how the protagonist is tempted and by sin brought low, even to despair: the desperate need for the rite must be demonstrated, as it were, so that the magnitude of God's grace and providence can be more effectively shown. Hence a great part of the fictional pattern involves the protagonist's confrontation with the world, the flesh, and the devil and the complications wrought by the resulting sin. On the other hand, the basic rite provides release from the sin and resolves the complications; it provides a denouement.

In *Paradise Lost* it is not until Book IX that Adam and Eve fall; they then suffer the complicating consequences of sin until the end of Book X; here they repent and confess their sins, and their confession is brought to the Father by

17

the Son early in Book XI; though divine justice must be satisfied, divine mercy is offered them; their sentence is commuted. Michael is sent to Eden to instruct the sinners, bearing mercy as he metes out justice. His instruction consists of visions furnished Adam and then simple narrations of what is to come. Each vision and each story in the narrative provides a lesson. After each one Adam is moved to praise or to thank God for the lesson. The best example is his ecstatic outburst following the announcement of the coming of Christ: "O Prophet of glad tidings, finisher / Of utmost hope!" Then he utters his own *Ave Maria*:

> Virgin Mother, Hail,
> High in the love of Heav'n, yet from my Loins
> Thou shalt proceed, and from thy Womb the Son
> Of God most High; So God with man unites. (XII, 375-82)

After receiving instruction, Adam and Eve, cleansed and wiser now and with peace in their hearts, may hopefully face the world lying all before them. After Eve's "consolation" (XII, 610-23), the two move out of Eden in formal recessional: "High in Front advanc'd, / The brandisht Sword of God before them blaz'd / Fierce as a Comet," Michael leading them. The last two books create a liturgical pattern and serve a liturgical purpose—the assertion of God's providence and the affirmation of His covenant. Thus, the poet, unwittingly or not, has provided the historical original of liturgy and its basic design. Its cleansing power and the affirmation it affords are akin, as the poet knew, to the purging effect of Greek tragedy and served a similar if not identical function.[4]

As he knew also, the invocation of the Muse was not unakin to the preacher's prayer before his sermon. He had indicated as much as early as the Nativity Ode. Thinking of his hymn in that poem as the oblation of the prophet-priest, he called upon the Muse to join with the Angel Choir her voice touched with fire from off Isaiah's sacred altar. Before reading the Gospel at Mass the Catholic priest to this day, prostrate, prays that his lips and heart may be cleansed as

18

Isaiah's were. It is an obvious sort of formulary[5] and one readily adapted for the prayer before the sermon. In *Paradise Lost* Milton likewise united the classical invocation of the poet and the Christian invocation of the priest. The "modern style" of preaching, generally practiced in the Elizabethan and Jacobean era, required as a beginning a statement of theme, exordium, prayer, and then the entrance into the theme. The exordium or protheme or antetheme often were omitted.[6] Men's first disobedience and its consequence is the subject and out of scripture suggests the theme. The call upon the Heavenly Muse of Oreb or Sinai that inspired the prophet Moses is similar to the invocation of the classical poet. But this call is the prayer of the preacher:

> And chiefly Thou O Spirit, that dost prefer
> Before all Temples th' upright heart and pure,
> Instruct me, for Thou know'st; Thou from the first
> Wast present, and with mighty wings outspread
> Dove-like satst brooding on the vast Abyss
> And mad'st it pregnant: What in me is dark
> Illumine, what is low raise and support;
> That to the height of this great Argument
> I may assert Eternal Providence,
> And justify the ways of God to men. (I, 17-26)

Just such a formulary was spoken or should have been spoken by anyone beginning his sermon, his great argument. Each of the other invocations of the poem reveal the same care. It is the Celestial Light Milton calls upon to "shine inward" at the opening of Book III; the Heavenly Urania, "The meaning, not the Name," the "Heav'nly born" who did converse with Eternal Wisdom, at the opening of Book VII; and at the opening of Book IX his "Celestial Patroness" who dictates to him slumbering the "argument / Not less but more Heroic." He prays not so much that the Muse speak through him as that his heart and mind be purified so that his lips may speak the truth as delivered. Now a sermon is in itself neither ritual nor liturgy, but it may be fitted into liturgy, and it may become ritualistic. As the proper means

19

for religious expression many Puritans believed that neither liturgy nor official homily could be substituted for it; in fact, many thought official homily and liturgy should be supplanted by sermon and extempore prayer. Yet the sermon, both at its beginning and at its ending, retained the form, at least, of ritual: the call to action and a consolation or *ad gloriam Dei* usually ended the discourse. The four invocations in *Paradise Lost*, then, would call for four proper closings, or at least suggestions of them. Except for the ending of Book III, preceding the second invocation, the call for action is expressed and at least the suggestion of one or more of the formularies. At the end of Book VI Raphael turns the description of the Son's return triumphant from his defeat of Satan into a sort of *ad gloriam Dei*:

> he celebrated rode
> Triumphant through mid Heav'n, into the Courts
> And Temple of his mighty Father Thron'd
> On high; who into Glory him receiv'd,
> Where he now sits at the right hand of bliss. (VI, 888-92)

He then in the very last lines warns Adam about the proper action to follow. At the end of Book VIII, preceding the final invocation and following Raphael's second set of instructions, exhortations, and final warnings about proper action, Adam says farewell to him in what is called a "benediction." It is possible that Milton here is consciously, but properly, giving the benediction to the instructed, the hearer, and ringing a change on the use of the little ritual. At the end of Book XII, Michael calls upon Adam to "add / Deeds to thy knowledge answerable; add Faith, / Add Virtue, Patience, Temperance, add Love." So adding, he will "possess / A Paradise within thee, happier far," and so will Eve, as we are told. The *applicatio* has been brilliantly blended with the *pax vobiscum*. So ends the sermon before the closing recessional. It seems quite possible that Milton thought of these customary forms as he wrote of the beginning of things—even of how sermons got started—for he was well aware of the ways of the preacher.[7]

He was equally aware of the priestly office, as these invocations will also indicate. If the Heavenly Muse who inspired Moses is Urania, that which prefers the upright heart and pure is certainly the same spirit called upon at the ordination service of the priest. The concern of critics to identify this spirit with the divine light who sits with Spenser's Sapience, or with St. Augustine's light which God has made, or with other lights, physical or divine,[8] seems an unnecessary hunt for what is assumed to be hidden. The rather obvious identification, and the one not hitherto recognized, is that Creator Spiritus called upon in the great Pentecostal hymn sung at every service of ordination of a priest or at every consecration of a bishop, whether Roman or Anglican. It apparently goes back to the ninth century. As H. T. Henry observes,[9] it is the one hymn out of the splendid Latin hymnody of the Roman Church retained in the liturgy of the Church of England, which is a tribute to the power of the piece. It fits Milton's occasion so remarkably well he could hardly have avoided echoing it, or for that matter the prayers of the ordination service. A few stanzas of the Latin will be sufficient to illustrate the echo (I quote from Henry's version):

> Veni, Creator Spiritus,
> Mentes tuorum visita,
> Imple superna gratia
> Quae tu creasti pectora.
>
> Qui diceris Paraclitus,
> Altissimi donum Dei,
> Fons vivus, ignis, charitas,
> Et spiritalis unctio.
>
> Accende lumen sensibus,
> Infunde amorem cordibus,
> Infirma nostri corporis
> Virtute firmans perpeti.

21

The various English translations are variously garbled, but all set forth the basic meaning. That same Spirit which made the vast abyss pregnant is Creator Spirit, and that Spirit will descend upon the poet-priest to illumine his creative mind as he assumes his ministry. As the most high gift of God, it will raise and support him, will shine inward and irradiate his mind, and will bring to him eternal wisdom. The Creator Spirit, in the hymn also called the Paraclete, the Comforter, and the Ordination rite calls down the Holy Ghost upon the ordinand. Whether or not this is the same spirit who descends as a dove upon Jesus after his baptism—and Milton in the *Christian Doctrine* rather doubts its being the Holy Ghost—it is certainly that Creator Spirit who is called upon to illuminate the mind of Milton the priest. The poet intends his reader to make the identification, even though he himself may have reservations about following the hymn's identification of the Spirit with the Holy Ghost. The Invocations serve both the preacher and the priest.

More apparent than the ritualistic and liturgical patterns suggested by the poem as a whole are the liturgical and ritualistic embryons developing within its parts. Set in Hell and Chaos, the action in Books I and II would hardly be expected to yield much by way of religious rite and ceremony: the one is a perverse and pagan place, and the other entirely disorderly. The paganism of Hell perverts its ceremonies and rites, and the disorder of Chaos prevents them altogether. A nice example is Satan's perversion of the familiar salutation to the dead, *Ave atque vale*, originally from Catullus' monody at the grave of his brother. Satan uses it as the ritual for claiming possession of Hell, his new kingdom, but emphasizes his perversion by reversing the words. His becomes a *Vale atque ave*:

> Farewell happy fields
> Where Joy for ever dwells: Hail horrors, hail
> Infernal world, and thou profoundest Hell
> Receive thy new Possessor: One who brings

A mind not to be chang'd by Place or Time.
The mind is its own place, and in itself
Can make a Heav'n of Hell, a Hell of Heav'n. (I, 249-55)

Now a Christian monarch or conqueror would take possession of a new realm in the name of God, claim it as God's viceregent, and be anointed and crowned in a religious ceremony; he would not salute and possess it in the formal words of a well-known salute to the dead—or to death. The irony is increased by Satan's farewell to joy and his welcome to horror. The same can be said of the passage if it was intended to suggest—and Milton probably intended it to—another familiar quotation from a pagan ritual: *Ave, Imperator, morituri te salutamus,* the words spoken by the gladiators, as Suetonius tells us, when they entered the arena. To salute Caesar was to salute death. The perverted religious nature of Satan's formal salutation and seizure of Hell is made yet more apparent and the irony more intense by the heresy of the unchangeable and self-sufficient mind with which Satan immediately follows the words of salutation, a heresy that sometimes traps readers of the poem. Actually, the passage is the rite by which he arrogantly renounces true life and desperately embraces a living death.

Toward the end of Book I the winged heralds of Satan's host proclaim "with awful Ceremony / And Trumpets' sound" the council to be held in Pandemonium, and there the "great consult" is held, the account of which takes up the first half of Book II. This assembly with its debates is, of course, a military and political affair, a travesty of a parliament, but it is held in a ceremonious manner, each of the speeches following in general the form of a classical oration and revealing the character of the speaker. Pandemonium, "Built like a Temple," resembles not merely the vast temples to oriental deities including Solomon's, but with its arched ceiling and vast spaces, the splendor of St. Peter's itself. And the whole meeting there has its overtones of perverted religious ritual. As the Christian worshipper comes into the

23

church despairing because of his sin, so Satan and his "thousand Demi-Gods" sit upon their golden seats in deepest despair. But Satan's despair is perverted. It has lifted him and his forces beyond hope; or to put it differently, when total despair has possessed them and they have made their commitment to it, when there is no longer any turning back and all hope is irrecoverably lost, he becomes utterly reckless, "From despair / Thus uplifted beyond hope." Throughout the debate—which is contrastingly paralleled by the meeting in Heaven in Book III—the cleansing of the stain of despair does not take place, but rather it is fed. Such accommodation with despair might have been made, except for Satan and Beelzebub, whose insatiate desire prevailed. Satan and all his chiefs leave the meeting not purged or cleansed, but rather worse stained, more bloated, and more filthy than they came. Furthermore, the meeting ends in an idolatrous ceremony, with all Satan's followers bowing down and throwing themselves prone before him: "Towards him they bend / With awful reverence prone; and as a God / Extol him equal to the highest in Heav'n" (II, 477-79). It is a travesty of the scene in the following Book, in which the hosts of Heaven

> lowly reverent
> Towards either Throne they bow, and to the ground
> With solemn adoration down they cast
> Thir Crowns inwove with Amarant and Gold. (III, 349-52)

Idolatry also prevails in the state procession which follows. In it the grand infernal peers come out in formal and proper order, in their midst "Hell's dread Emperor with pomp Supreme, / And God-like imitated state." The whole scene is to be contrasted with the final scene in Pandemonium in Book X. Hell's triumphant emperor and pontifex maximus is met by his hosts in like pomp and splendor. He makes his report and his vaunt and formally proffers this new world to his followers. He expects loud acclaim, prostrations before him, and great adulation. His followers do fall prone before him, but as serpents writhing and groveling in ashes, uttering not applause but "A dismal universal hiss." A ceremony of praise has turned into a rite of derision. The last meeting in Pandemonium is the product of the first, and the idolatry of the first becomes a burlesque of that ceremony in the last.

Like the council in Hell, the first council of Heaven has ceremonial if not liturgical overtones and is more distinctly religious. In contrast to the hollow rhetoric, the satire, and the vaunting of the lengthy infernal debate followed by idolatrous ritual, the Father's formal, straightforward pronouncements and the Son's quiet offer of himself meekly as sacrifice for the sins of the whole world, followed by the hymn of the angels in Book III, are formal expressions of utter sincerity and devotion. They provide the means for salvation, thereby foreshadowing the action of Book XI and laying the foundation for the sacrament instituted there. The pronouncements are made while ambrosial fragrance as incense fills Heaven. The explanation that "in him [the Son] all his father shone / Substantially express'd," and the Father's statement that the Son is "My word, my wisdom, and effectual might," echo the Nicene Creed: "Begotten, not made; Being of one substance with the Father; By whom all things were made: Who for us men and for our salvation came down from heaven, And was incarnate by the Holy Ghost of the Virgin Mary, and was made man." They also reflect the more elaborate statement of the doctrine of the Logos as found in the first fourteen verses of the Fourth Gospel, themselves anciently a part of ritual, being adapted by the Holy Apostle from one of the sapiential psalms and used in the Book of Common Prayer as the Gospel for Christmas Day. The statement that the Son's imputed merit absolves those

> who renounce
> Thir own both righteous and unrighteous deeds,
> And live in thee transplanted, and from thee
> Receive new life (III, 291-94)

incorporates the doctrine though not the words of the Prayer of Humble Access of the Lord's Supper, "that we may euermore dwell in him and he in vs," and it anticipates a fuller development of the doctrine in the rite performed in Book XI.

The Son having taken upon Himself man's guilt, the Father makes Him "Head Supreme" and "Anointed universal king" and bestows upon Him all power in formal declaration, calling upon all in Heaven to worship and adore Him. Whereupon the multitude of angels, as Milton had learned from the Book of Revelation, bow before each throne and cast down their golden crowns before the two. They then introduce their "sacred Song" to honor and praise the Father and the Son. This hymn is actually an elaborated *Gloria Patri*, the Holy Spirit being omitted as apparently not having yet proceeded from the Father and the Son. The Father's character and the Son's character and deeds—for the Son had already driven Satan out of Heaven—are celebrated. At the end they sing,

> Hail Son of God, Savior of Men, thy Name
> Shall be the copious matter of my Song
> Henceforth, and never shall my Harp thy praise
> Forget, nor from thy Father's praise disjoin. (III, 412-15)

From this time onward the Son's name must be always associated with the Father's in all expression of praise. Glory must be to the Father *and* to the Son. So it is that the Son was anointed and properly enthroned in religious ritual in Heaven. And in his elevation the words and music come, not from Scripture only, but from theological essentials reiterated in the Scriptural words of church liturgy. They suggest the origins of such liturgy and rites, in that the events here recorded took place even before the Fall.

Eve's account of her first remembrances recorded in Book IV likewise sets forth the original of yet another rite, the marriage ceremony. No priestly angel such as Raphael comes down from Heaven to perform the actual ceremony, but the Son, the Creator-God Himself, invisible, leads Eve on to Adam. By so doing He institutes this honorable state,

as the marriage rite of the Book of Common Prayer tells us
He did. God's holy ordinance it may be, but the words for
Milton belong only to those who enter the covenant, and
these words echo the Biblical account of that first ceremony
in Eden. It is a natural marriage requiring only the guidance
of the invisible spirit of God, for they are already one flesh:
subsequent marriages will require only such explanation of
this union as seems necessary.[10] Under the Plantan tree, as
Eve remembers, Adam had pronounced unpremeditated the
ceremony:

> Return fair *Eve*,
> Whom fli'st thou? whom thou fli'st, of him thou art,
> His flesh, his bone; to give thee being I lent
> Out of my side to thee, nearest my heart
> Substantial Life, to have thee by my side
> Henceforth an individual solace dear;
> Part of my Soul I seek thee, and thee claim
> My other half: with that thy gentle hand
> Seiz'd mine, I yielded, and from that time see
> How beauty is excell'd by manly grace
> And wisdom, which alone is truly fair. (IV, 481-91)

The emphasis here, as it was in Milton's prose, is upon the
solace and companionship provided by a marriage based upon
the natural affinity of souls and the natural superiority and
leadership of the husband. It carries in it the substance of
the instructions given following the vows in the marriage
ceremony of the Elizabethan Book of Common Prayer: "So
men are bounde to love their owne wyues, as their owne
bodies. He that loueth his owne wife loueth hym selfe. For
neuer did any man hate his owne fleshe."

The same emphasis occurs in the account of the wedding
that Adam gives Raphael in Book VIII. Overjoyed at his
first sight of Eve, he thanks God for his companion, the
fairest of all God's gifts, and repeats from the Wedding
Ceremony the injunction, Biblical in origin, that the wedded
pair shall leave father and mother and, forsaking all others,
cleave only to each other:

I now see

Bone of my Bone, Flesh of my Flesh, my Self
Before me; Woman is her Name, of Man
Extracted; for this cause he shall forgo
Father and Mother, and to his Wife adhere;
And they shall be one Flesh, one Heart, one Soul.

(VIII, 494-99)

Having wooed her, he led Eve, blushing, into the nuptial bower, where the winds whispered, the birds sang, and from their wings flung rose.

The wedding ceremony is not the only rite associated with the marriage. A part of it are those rites leading up to the consummation. As the wedded pair toward evening move on to their nuptial bower, "heav'nly Choirs the Hymenaean sung." Then, after their Evensong, the poet breaks in with his own epithalamion, a hymn to chaste love beginning: "Hail wedded Love, mysterious Law, true source / Of human offspring, sole propriety / In Paradise of all things common else" (IV, 751-53). Finally the nightingale, whose "amorous descant" has been going on the while in the background, lulls the pair asleep. If the form of the wedding ceremony is so casual and "natural" as to seem pagan, the pagan consummation rites have been so transformed as to seem utterly Christian in both form and meaning.

But before the epithalamion, before all the marriage rites are done and in a sense a part of them, the couple sing their Evensong. It is a noble canticle involving thanks, petition, and praise. The petition is merely implied, of course, for Milton maintained that God knows man's needs before man can know them: it simply reminds God of his promise of offspring and thus serves the function of the prayer for children found in the wedding liturgy of the church. But Adam and Eve's extempore canticle serves also the function of the Prayer Book's Evensong and echoes its canticles and prayers. As the two arrive at their bower, they turn and adore God the creator of all the spacious firmament, then chant these lines:

Thou also mad'st the Night,
Maker Omnipotent, and thou the Day,
Which we in our appointed work imploy'd
Have finish happy in our mutual help
And mutual love, the Crown of all our bliss
Ordain'd by thee, and this delicious place
For us too large, where thy abundance wants
Partakers, and uncropt falls to the ground.
But thou hast promis'd from us two a Race
To fill the earth, who shall with us extol
Thy goodness infinite, both when we wake,
And when we seek, as now, thy gift of sleep. (IV, 724-35)

Professor Hughes has observed rightly that this passage echoes Psalms lxxiv and cxxvii.[11] He has not observed that according to the Calendar, both these Psalms are appointed to be read or chanted at Evening Prayer, nor has he observed that Psalms xcviii and lxvii were used as canticles for Evening Prayer in Elizabeth's Prayer Book and that in word, doctrine, or imagery contribute either to the adoration or to the hymn itself. In the one we are asked to "singe vnto the Lord a newe songe," just such a song as Adam and Eve were to sing, "for he hath done marueilous thinges." In the other the people are admonished to praise the Lord, for "Then shall the earth bringe foorth her increase, and God, euen our owne God, shall geue vs his blessinge." The last two lines remind us of the Second Collect at Evening Prayer: that we "may passe our time in rest and quietnes."

The poet makes complex where most he would seem to simplify. He reduces, modifies, consolidates, and at times merely suggests; yet he expects his reader to realize a rite as such. For in the very next lines he comments: "This said unanimous, and other rites / Observing none, but adoration pure / Which God likes best, into thir inmost bower / Handed they went." Spontaneous and inspired though it may be by the occasion, it is yet a formal expression, a ceremonial act, a rite with echoes enough from established liturgy to make its identity unmistakable; indeed it is the imaginary reconstruction of the original of Evening Prayer.

29

After the birds have shrilled their "Matin Song" at the opening of Book V and after Adam has, to waken her, whispered his imitation of the Song of Solomon into Eve's ear, the newly spoused say their Morning Prayer. The poet writes the rubrics for the service and explains again that the canticle itself, which is again the rite, comes "unmeditated" from their lips:

> Lowly they bow'd adoring, and began
> Their Orisons, each Morning duly paid
> In various style, for neither various style
> Nor holy rapture wanted they to praise
> Thir Maker, in fit strains pronounct or sung
> Unmeditated. (V, 144-49)

In spite of our first parents' acknowledged extempore ability, however, the recorder of their pristine prayers allowed them to anticipate in their liturgy a part of the liturgy for Morning Prayer developed out of Scripture—out of the Apocrypha indeed. For as others have observed, Adam and Eve based their hymn to Creation rather directly upon the Song of the Three Holy Children as deleted from the third chapter of Daniel and placed, because it has come down to us in the Greek rather than the Hebrew, in the Protestant Apocrypha. The Children's Canticle is actually in two parts, and forms two canticles in the Order for Morning Prayer in the present Prayer Book, the first being known as the *Benedictus es, Domine* and the second, a very long canticle, as the *Benedicite, omnia opera Domini*. Its noncanonical position did not prevent the latter's being incorporated from earlier liturgies into Morning Prayer in Elizabeth's Prayer Book.[12] Although Milton may have drawn his exaltation of the Father in the firmament of Heaven from the first, he begins as the second begins with the works of the Lord which are called upon to bless Him forever. Then Milton's hymn calls upon all of God's creatures to praise their Creator and in proper order, much as the Canticle does, ranging from the heavenly hierarchies downward to the fish and all that creep the earth.

To any who read, the similarity is obvious, as a sample will demonstrate: "O all ye worckes of the Lorde, bless ye the Lorde: Praise him, and magnify him for euer," the Canticle begins. It then calls upon the angels of God to bless Him, then the heavens, the waters above the firmament, the sun and moon and stars, the showers and dew, the winds, the fire and heat, winter and summer, frost and cold, ice and snow, nights and days, light and darkness, then the earth, the mountains and hills, and all the green things upon the earth, the wells and seas and floods, the whales and fishes, the fowls and beasts of the field, and then the Children of Men.

Adam and Eve's hymn begins: "These are thy glorious works, Parent of good, / Almighty, thine this universal Frame, / Thus wondrous fair" (V, 153-55). It then calls upon "ye sons of Light, Angels," then all in Heaven and Earth to join in choral symphonies to praise the Lord. As Professor Joseph H. Summers has shown in his excellent analysis of this hymn,[13] following the general statement, it becomes, as did the Canticle, more and more particular as it ranges generally down the scale of being: from the morning star to the sun and moon, to the fixed stars and the planets, to light and darkness, to the air and the other elements, to the mists and exhalations, to the clouds and their showers, to the four winds of the earth, to the pines, the fountains, the birds, the waters that glide, to every living thing that walks or creeps the earth, and finally to Adam and Eve, mankind. In purpose the two are the same and in pattern and in particulars they are much alike. Milton is careful, however, to avoid anachronism: he does not allow Adam and Eve, for example, to call upon the harsher aspects of nature, such as ice and snow, to celebrate their Maker. Similarly, he cannot make use of the last section of the canticle which calls upon the Children of Men, Israel, and the souls of the righteous to praise the Lord. Furthermore, in keeping with the rest of his poem, he has maintained the simplicity of his style, allowing Adam and Eve no choruses or refrains, such as characterize the Canticle. He marks the

31

disguise of his ritual just enough to make certain that it is recognized and identified for the rite it is. This rite, or one very similar, is used again, for on the next day at dawn Adam and Eve join their "vocal Worship to the Choir / Of Creatures wanting voice," as morning incense rises from "Earth's great Altar" (IX, 192-200).

Hardly a rite, Eve's plans for the dinner with Raphael establish for future generations the proper rules for arranging a meal, especially the selection of the proper sequence of foods: "on hospitable thought intent" she contrives the proper order of foods so "as not to mix / Tastes, not well join'd, inelegant, but bringing / Taste upheld with change" (V, 332-36). Although not exactly religious, the meal yet begins with an unpremeditated grace spoken by Adam and by the Archangel. Unrecognized by most, the natural rite emerges, unrecognized also by those who instituted it as a proper custom. Yet it is again marked sufficiently by the diction to indicate the poet's intention:

> Heav'nly stranger, please to taste
> These bounties which our Nourisher, from whom
> All perfect good unmeasur'd out, descends,
> To us for food and for delight hath caus'd
> The Earth to yield;
>
> .   .   .   .   .
>
> To whom the Angel. Therefore what he gives
> (Whose praise be ever sung) to man in part
> Spiritual, may of purest Spirits be found
> No ingrateful food. (V, 397-407)

Such words and phrases echo the graces to be said before meat as set forth in Lily's Latin Grammar and in the numerous primers and books of devotion of the sixteenth and seventeenth centuries: "These bounties," "our Nourisher," "from whom / All perfect good," "hath caus'd / The Earth to yield." For example, in a "Grace before Dyner" in the Grafton Primer one finds: "Good lorde bless us and al they gyftes, which we receiue they bounteous liberalitie."[14] In John Knox's "Prayers etc. Subjoyned to Calvin's Catechism" is a "Prayer to be Said before Meales," in which one finds "so that hereby we may acknowledge thee to be the author and giver of all good things."[15] In Thomas Becon's *The Governance of Virtue* a "Prayer Before Dinner" asks that God "bless us and all these thy gifts, which we at this present shall receive of thy bounteous hand."[16] So the first grace before dinner comes naturally from the lips of the first man, whose words anticipate, the poet would have us believe, succeeding proper expressions of the rite here established.[17]

While yet Eve is planning her meal, another ceremony takes place, another piece of liturgy anticipated. Adam greets and invites Raphael to the dinner in simple but ceremonious words, and Raphael accepts in like words. As the two then come to the "Silvan Lodge" they meet Eve

> On whom the Angel *Hail*
> Bestow'd, the holy salutation us'd
> Long after to blest *Mary*, second *Eve*.
>   Hail Mother of Mankind, whose fruitful Womb
> Shall fill the World more numerous with thy Sons
> Than with these various fruits the Trees of God
> Have heap'd this Table. (V, 385-91)

Even the *Ave Maria* is anticipated in the pre-lapsarian world and used for the same purpose, the announcement of offspring.

Another, and the very next, religious ritual and liturgical passage is likewise to be associated with "blest Mary." It is the canticle sung by the Angels following the Father's commissioning of the Son to take "My overshadowing Spirit" and create the heavens and the earth, to shape them out of the boundless deep. It is based primarily upon the *Gloria in excelsis*, the hymn sung by the Herald Angels at the Nativity, itself the noblest act of creation, and always associated with the Virgin. But it also seems to be associated with her hymn, the *Magnificat*, at the time of the Annunciation. The *Gloria in excelsis* always was said or sung at the end of the Lord's Supper as required by Queen Elizabeth's Prayer Book and the *Magnificat* at Evening Prayer.[18] Milton records these as the words the angels sung:

> Glory they sung to the most High, good will
> To future men, and in their dwellings peace:
> Glory to him whose just avenging ire
> Had driven out th' ungodly from his sight
> And th' habitations of the just; to him
> Glory and praise, whose wisdom had ordain'd
> Good out of evil to create, instead
> Of Spirits malign a better Race to bring
> Into their vacant room, and thence diffuse
> His good to Worlds and Ages infinite. (VII, 182-91)

The opening lines here are essentially the familiar opening lines of the *Gloria in excelsis*: "Glorye be to God on hyghe. And in earthe peace, good wyll towardes men." The next lines, celebrating the expulsion of Satan and his proud forces from Heaven, suggest the last lines of the *Magnificat*. In these the Virgin rejoices in the elevation, to be brought about by the Annunciation, from her lowliness to become "second Eve" and the means for God's keeping the covenant with Abraham. Out of the basic evil, out of her original sin, shall come the good of her Son, the salvation of mankind. Magnified by the Lord, purified as the perfect vessel, she becomes the means for the supreme example of God's turning evil into good. These are her pertinent lines:

> He hath shewed strength with his arme; he hath scatered the proude in the imagination of their hertes.
> He hath put downe the mightye from theyr seate; and hath exalted the humble and meke. . . .
> He remembering his mercy, hath holpen his seruaunte Israel: as he promysed to our forefathers, Abraham and his sede for euer.

In *Paradise Lost* God the Son has already scattered the proud in the imagination of their hearts. He will now come down from Heaven to create a world and a better race than the self-corrupted spirits now expelled. The hymn heralding His coming foreshadows His later coming to create through Mary a race redeemed. And Milton's song for the angels, echoing the words of the first earthly service of praise and thanksgiving offered the Son, in a sense affirms the liturgical paradigm established. Yet "The meaning, not the Name I call"; and though like occasions ask like forms, the poet would remind us that occasions are never identical. Hence, variety in expression and great freedom within form.

Earlier, in Book VI, for example, the occasion of the Son's triumphant return from His overthrow of Satan called for no religious service or canticles of angelic praise. On the contrary, silent the heavenly hosts in awe watched the triumphal military procession. "To create," the angels explain, "Is greater than created to destroy." So it is the occasion of the Son's return from the Creation which prompts one of the greatest of the angelic canticles, perhaps the most appropriate of all. He rides up to his throne acclaimed by the symphonious sound of ten thousand harps. The earth and air resounded as he came. "The Heav'ns and all the Constellations rung, / The Planets and thir station list'ning stood, / While the bright Pomp ascended jubilant" (VII, 562-64). Following the procession with its great music, the angels sang their canticle, a celebration of the Creation, a consecration of the world:

> Open, ye everlasting Gates, they sung,
> Open, ye Heav'ns, your living doors; let in
> The great Creator from his work return'd
> Magnificent, his Six days' work, a World;
> Open, and henceforth oft; for God will deign
> To visit oft the dwellings of just Men
> Delighted, and with frequent intercourse
> Thither will send his winged Messengers
> On errands of supernal Grace. (VII, 565-73)

Certainly as early as the ninth century, perhaps even earlier, verses from Psalm xxiv were used as the dramatic introduction to the rite of the consecration of a church—indeed those same verses Milton paraphrases here. The bishop leading a procession comes to the portals of the newly built church, knocks on the doors, and calls for them to be opened. As soon as someone from inside answers and opens them, the bishop sweeps in at the head of his procession, all chanting Psalm cxxii.[19] In 1620, Bishop Lancelot Andrewes drew up the most famous and influential of Consecration forms; and although it was widely and extensively used, it was never adopted and placed in the Prayer Book by the English Church, nor has any other been. Milton in all probability knew Andrewes' rite, as well as those preceding it, all of which begin with Psalm xxiv. The Psalm is still used in the Roman rite. The American branch, the Episcopal Church, begins the consecration with the bishop leading a procession from the door down the aisle, all chanting or repeating antiphonally Psalm xxiv.[20] It was by design, we can be sure, that Milton repeats the familiar words of the ancient rite. He also expected his readers to regard them as a rite, or at least the *leitmotif* of a rite—the proper form for consecrating the newly-built world. This world must be consecrated, for God and his angels will visit it frequently and be at home in it, as they are in His church.

But the ceremony celebrating the Son's return from Creation was not the end of the occasion. On the seventh day He rested, and on this first sabbath a supreme service of praise and thanksgiving was sung in Heaven. The harp, the dulcimer, the organ, and all the other instruments of Heaven were tuned and intermixed with angel voices to sing the six days' acts. The hymn begins:

> Great are thy works, *Jehovah*, infinite
> Thy power; what thought can measure thee or tongue
> Relate thee; greater now in thy return
> Than from the Giant Angels; thee that day
> Thy Thunders magnifi'd; but to create
> Is greater than created to destroy. (VII, 602-607)

It goes on to celebrate the putting down of the apostate angels, the shaping of the vast world with its numerous stars,

36

and the creation of man in His own image to rule over His works. The empyrean rang with *Halleluiahs*, as it did in the Revelation vouchsafed to John of Patmos. Perhaps, though, the angels' hymn owes as much to a canticle to be sung at Evening Prayer, Psalm xcviii, as it does to Revelation iv, v, or xix. The canticle begins "O singe vnto the Lorde a newe songe: for he hath done marueilous thinges. With his owne right hande, and with his holy arme: hath he gotten him selfe the victory." So were the apostates put down, much as Milton's angels sing "easily the proud attempt / Of Spirits apostate and their Counsels vain / Thou hast repell'd." Later in the canticle all the lands are called upon to show themselves joyful unto the Lord and to praise him upon the harp and with trumpets and shawns and voices. Milton's hymn may also owe something to the *Venite* of Morning Prayer, Psalm xcv, a canticle which celebrates the greatness of God and the vastness of his creation. In it men are asked to come and to sing praises unto the Lord, for He is a great God who holds the corners of the earth in his hands, who made the sea and the dry land, and before whom all the earth must stand in awe. Or when Milton wrote he may well have remembered yet another canticle from the Prayer Book, the *Jubilate Deo* of Morning Prayer, Psalm c. In this Psalm all lands are called upon to be joyful in the Lord, for He is their creator and the creator of all men, and they are His people, the race of worshippers mentioned by Milton's angels. Canticles and hymn alike emphasize God's putting down Satan and the forces of evil, His creation of the world and of man, and man's obligation to worship and to thank Him. Likewise, the "amplitude immense" of the imagery of both argues Milton's awareness of these parts of liturgy as he wrote his own account of the origin of a liturgy.[21]

At the end of Book VIII Adam's farewell to Raphael, following the angel's admonition, is called a "benediction", a suggestion perhaps of nothing more than Milton's concern that leavetakings should be of such good words as to carry the religious overtones of blessings. Milton takes, though not for liturgical purposes, words from liturgy most appropriate to his need early in Book IX. Satan has lately fled Eden when Gabriel finds him in shape of a toad at Eve's ear; he now returns to his attack "improv'd / In meditated fraud and malice, bent / On Man's destruction" (IX, 54-56). The Collect for The Visitation of the Sick in Elizabeth's Prayer Book carries this petition for the sick person: "Renue in him most louyng father whatsouer hath been decaied, by the fraud, and malice of the deuel, or by his owne carnall will." It is Satan's fraud and malice in both cases, and the passage illustrates very well how the poet's sensitive ear picks the proper phrase, even from the less well known liturgies.[22]

Satan's improvement in fraud and malice is realized dramatically in Eve's first act following her eating the fruit: she pays idolatrous devotion to the tree, worshipping not God but what God had made:

> So saying, from the Tree her step she turn'd,
> But first low Reverence done, as to the power
> That dwelt within, whose presence had infus'd
> Into the plant sciential sap, deriv'd
> From Nectar, drink of Gods. (IX, 834-38)

As her eating the fruit was corrupt and corrupting, so was her ceremony perverted. The low reverence, possibly a genuflexion, was intended to be associated, no doubt, with papistry. Milton seems to be at pains to distinguish the genuine from the false and to define the danger of being innocently entrapped by empty forms.

The consequence of the entrapment is made evident in still another formal or ritualistic section. Early in Book X we are told that the Son comes down to Eden to try and to pass judgment upon the fallen ones. The trial is simple and consists of admissions of guilt, the absence of the Serpent being proof of his guilt. But the judgment is more formal, more complicated and more subtle: it involves an observation of the guilt of each, a sentence of each, curses, and the final sentence or judgment of death. One is reminded that a formal curse was still retained in the Elizabethan Prayer Book as the opening section of A Commination Against Sinners, a part of liturgy. The Son, formally judging the Serpent guilty of corrupting Adam and Eve, curses him and sentences him to grovel on his belly eternally, to eat dust, and to have his head bruised by the seed of the Woman. The Woman, admitting her guilt, must bear her children in pain and be subservient to her husband. Because Adam is guilty of harkening to his wife, the ground for him is curst and also

> In the sweat of thy Face shalt thou eat Bread,
> Till thou return unto the ground, for thou
> Out of the ground wast taken, know thy Birth,
> For dust thou art, and shalt to dust return. (**X**, 205-208)

Throughout the entire passage Milton quotes verbatim from Genesis iii, especially these last lines. But the last one of all, and the last words the Son was ever to speak to Adam and Eve, had their most familiar place in the Order for the Burial of the Dead. Like the liturgists before him, Milton built his original rite out of Scriptures, reflecting other rites akin to his so that they will be properly recognized as rites.

Toward the end of Book X, Eve, with broken and contrite heart, falls humbly at Adam's feet and assumes the guilt for the original sin. Her confession to him, especially in its repetition of the pronoun of the first person, distinctly echoes the *Confiteor*, anciently used in several liturgies, but chiefly by priest and acolytes at the beginning of the Mass or the Communion Service. As the acolytes prostrate themselves before the altar at the feet of the priest to confess to God, the saints, and the priest, so Eve prostrates herself at Adam's feet to confess, as required by Milton's hierarchical system, to her priest-husband: she to God through him.

> On me exercise not
> Thy hatred for this misery befall'n,
> On me already lost, mee than thyself
> More miserable; both have sinn'd, but thou
> Against God only, I against God and thee,

And to the place of judgment will return,
There with my cries importune Heaven, that all
The sentence from thy head remov'd may light
On me, sole cause to thee of all this woe,
Mee mee only just object of his ire. (X, 927-36)

The pertinent part of the *Confiteor* here is of course the familiar climax following the naming of the apostles and "omnibus sanctis, et tibi, Pater: / quia peccavi nimis cogitatione, verbo et opere: / mea culpa, mea culpa, mea maxima culpa." It seems altogether probable that the *Confiteor* was used in the English Church in Milton's day by some clergy as it is by some today.[23] However that may be, Milton is quite obviously remembering the familiar words as he writes and is making proper use of them; for this *confiteor*, bringing the pair to the place of judgment and to acknowledgment of their guilt, forms the first part of the poet's account of an adumbration of the Holy Sacrament.

The second part is largely a rubric. Eve's confession and penitence evoke Adam's forgiveness and his own penitence. The two then go to the place of their judgment. There, penitent, they prostrate themselves

Before him reverent, and both confess'd
Humbly thir faults, and pardon begg'd, with tears
Watering the ground, and with their sighs the Air
Frequenting, sent from hearts contrite, in sign
Of sorrow unfeign'd, and humiliation meek. (X, 1100-104)

The description suggests the priest's invitation to accompany him to the throne of the heavenly Grace in the General Confession: "but confesse them [our sins] with an humble, lowly, penitent, and obedient harte to the end that we may obtaine forgeuines of the same by his infinite goodnesse and mercie."

The rubric and description continue in the opening of Book XI. As the two stand praying, Prevenient Grace descends to remove "The Stony from thir hearts" and to make "new flesh / Regenerate grow instead." The Spirit of Prayer, faster than utterance itself, carries their sighs to Heaven. Then the scene is changed, or enlarged. Their prayers have moved Adam and Eve into the Real Presence, and the readers of the poem with them, as it were, await the canon of the Mass:

> To Heav'n thir prayers
> Flew up, nor miss'd the way, by envious winds
> Blown vagabond or frustrate: in they pass'd
> Dimensionless through Heav'nly doors: then clad
> With incense, where the Golden Altar fum'd,
> By thir great Intercessor, came in sight
> Before the Father's Throne: Them the glad Son
> Presenting, thus to intercede began.
> See Father, what first fruits on Earth are sprung
> From thy implanted Grace in Man, these Sighs
> And Prayers, which in this Golden Censer, mixt
> With Incense, I thy Priest before thee bring,
> Fruits of more pleasing savor from thy seed
> Sown with contrition in his heart, than those
> Which his own hands manuring all the Trees
> Of Paradise could have produc't, ere fall'n
> From innocence. Now therefore bend thine ear
> To supplication, hear his sighs though mute;
> Unskilful with what words to pray, let mee
> Interpret for him, mee his Advocate
> And propitiation, all his works on mee
> Good or not good ingraft, my Merit those
> Shall perfet, and for these my Death shall pay.
> Accept me, and in mee from these receive
> The smell of peace toward Mankind, let him live
> Before thee reconcil'd, at least his days
> Number'd, though sad, till Death, his doom (which I
> To mitigate thus plead, not to reverse)
> To better life shall yield him, where with mee
> All my redeem'd may dwell in joy and bliss,
> Made one with me as I with thee am one. (XI, 14-44)

The Son has interceded with His own body and as advocate and intercessor offered Himself. The Father at once accepts the offer: "All thy request for Man, accepted Son, / Obtain, all thy request was my decree." A little later (XI, 99-116) He

41

sends Michael not merely to carry out the mitigated sentence and to dismiss the fallen pair from Eden, but to dismiss them "not disconsolate," His covenant promised to be renewed in their seed. Man here has found grace as promised in Book III; the Son here has affirmed through his priestly act the covenant there made that He should give up His life for man. Here is the institution of a sacrament, for Milton held in the *Christian Doctrine* that sacraments are "given as tokens of the sealing of the covenant of grace and for the confirmation of our faith" (*Works*, XVI, 201). They "are given as a pledge or symbol to believers of the actual blessing" (*Works*, XVI, 219). And he also held that "a sacrament is a thing to be used, not abstained from: but a pledge, as it were, and memorial of obedience" (*Works*, XV, 115). The Lord's Supper, then, is an affirmation or reaffirmation of the grace once offered, and that offer was not first made in the upper chamber in Jerusalem or first confirmed there. For as we learn from the *Christian Doctrine*: "Even under the law the existence of a Redeemer and the necessity of redemption are perceptible, though obscurely." Or, as it is put a few lines later, "The manifestation of this gratuous covenant under the law was partly anterior to, and partly coincident with Moses" (*Works*, XVI, 103). So what is mentioned in the *Doctrine* is realized in the art of *Paradise Lost*.

And the realization is greatly enabled by other details of the art. It was not by chance merely that Milton made use of one—the last—of the "Comfortable Words" spoken by the priest following the Absolution in the Lord's Supper, for there were dozens of other Biblical texts equally satisfactory. His choice recalled at once the familiar ritual to the reader's mind and set forth his own understanding of Christ's sacerdotal function: "If any manne sinne, we haue an aduocate with the father, Jesus Christ the righteous, and he is the propiciation for our sinnes." In his discussion of the Lord's Supper in the *Christian Doctrine* he had said that "Christ is the sole priest of the new covenant" and cited the famous passage from Hebrews (vii, 23-24) as authority.[24] As the Son stands

42

interceding before "the Golden Altar fum'd" with incense, one must recall Albrecht Dürer's famous woodcut of St. Gregory's Mass, in which at the moment of consecration Christ comes alive from the retable of the altar, the walls and roof of the church fade, the golden cross becomes the true wooden cross, and two angels appear. In Milton's account, as in Gregory's miracle, the Presence is Real who can ordain for all who believe an absolution through His sacrifice once offered here. One must also recall a petition from the opening of the Prayer spoken by the priest for the Whole State of Christ's Church Militant Here on Earth: "we humbly beseche the most mercifully (to accepte our almose) and to receive these our prayers which we offer to thy diuine maiestie." But most important, one is reminded by the last line of the Son's intercession of the last petition of the Prayer of Humble Access, the prayer in Milton's time coming just before the Prayer of Consecration: "that we euermore dwell in him, and he in vs." The idea was repeated in the Oblation of the Edwardian Prayer Book and was restored in the Scottish Prayer Book of 1637: "And made one body with him, that he may dwell in them and they in him." Milton's line is a paraphrase of liturgy, not of the Scriptures. Though he was fully aware of the Biblical sources of the idea, when he came to elaborate the doctrine of being "ingrafted in Christ" in the *Christian Doctrine*, he said that believers "are made partakers of Christ, and meet for becoming one with him" (*Works*, XVI, 3). But also at the very outset of the ceremony before God's altar Prevenient Grace had descended and removed "The stony from thir hearts and made new flesh / Regenerate grow instead." Adam and Eve had already received some of the "benefits of His Passion." They may now, or their seed in future may, having partaken of His flesh, "euer hereafter serue and please the, in newenes of lyfe," as the Confession asks.

I am convinced that Milton intended this passage as an adumbration of the Lord's supper and that he expected his readers to recognize it as such. Professor Ross recognizes the pomp of the passage as "that very ritual which, presumably, is the mark of anti-Christ" and thinks Milton was here restricted by Raphael's doctrine of accommodation and was required to liken spiritual to corporal forms, for he contends that "Milton is the last man to intend a sacramental Catholic Heaven."[25] That the imagery of a few lines suggest the pomp of a high Mass may be true, and certainly Milton must use such language as will suggest the glories of heaven. The assumption, however, that he succeeds merely in suggesting anti-Christ is an error. The Lord's Supper, however, was quite another thing. Milton is following loosely the form of the liturgy as well as the meaning he knew and apparently accepted. Although not absolutely necessary to salvation, it was yet a means for reaffirming through the repentance it requires the covenant wrought through the Passion of the Son.

Artistically, it was something more. With the recognition of their sin and the admission of their guilt the albatross, as it were, falls from their necks and Adam and Eve can pray. Trust in God and His Providence—a theme basic to all Milton's major poems—is restored to them. That restoration is celebrated and affirmed in the ceremony before God's heavenly altar, and the denouement of the poem is provided. A Divine Comedy becomes possible. If the knotting of the plot comes with the eating of the apple in Eden—an unholy meal—the unknotting comes with the celebration in Heaven —the adumbration of the holy meal.

Hope and joy can now return to Eden: "new hope to spring / Out of despair, joy, but with fear linkt." With the dawn of a new day Adam and Eve have said their orisons (presumably not unlike those recorded earlier in their Morning Prayer), and a little later Adam sings his "Ave Eva," for peace has returned to his breast and to his memory the promise that Eve's offspring shall bruise the head of the Serpent:

> Hail to thee,
> *Eve* rightly call'd, Mother of all Mankind,

44

> Mother of all things living, since by thee
> Man is to live, and all things live for Man. (XI, 158-61)

The Morning Prayer is followed by a hymn of hope, for Eve is the chief source of hope. She in turn expresses herself formally in such words as became Mary, second Eve, when at the Annunciation Mary sang how God had "regarded the lowelines of his handmaiden," the *Magnificat* of Evening Prayer.

Since most of the remainder of the poem is made up of Michael's vision and narrative of the future, it could only awkwardly make a functional place for a rite or ceremony. Yet within his account occasionally come reflections of one, intimations which for the alert may enlarge and enrich meanings. Cain's and Abel's sacrifices illustrate, what all Scripture enjoins, that all sacrifices must be made "with meek heart and due reverence" and in sincerity. Cain obviously had come to his sacrifice without a truly penitent and obedient heart, bearing malice against his neighbor, without "a ful trust in Goddes mercy," and without "a quiet conscience," as were required by the Invitation to the Lord's Supper and by the several Exhortations in the Prayer Book. In Book XII Michael gives his account of Moses' establishing the Law. God comes down from the shaking top of Sinai and Himself in thunder, lightning, and trumpet's blast established them,

> part such as appertain
> To civil Justice, part religious Rites
> Of sacrifice, informing them, by types
> And shadows, of that destin'd Seed to bruise
> The Serpent, by what means he shall achieve
> Mankind's deliverance. (XII, 230-35)

Apparently, the religious rites of sacrifice are foreshadowings of later means, later symbols of sacrifice by which mankind may be delivered.

Finally, Michael elaborates a portion of the Creed, the actual quoted words being closer to the Nicene than to the

45

Apostles' Creed.[26] After the Son, so Michael foretells, has overcome Satan—a passage which suggests the harrowing of hell as provided for in the Apostles' Creed—He shall

> Then enter into glory, and resume
> His Seat at God's right hand, exalted high
> Above all names in Heav'n, and thence shall come,
> When this world's dissolution shall be ripe,
> With glory and power to judge both quick and dead,
> To judge th' unfaithful dead, but to reward
> His faithful.   (XII, 456-62)

The Nicene Creed states that Christ rose on the third day "And ascended into heaven, And sitteth on the right hand of the Father: And he [Christ] shall come again, with glory, to judge both the quick and the dead; Whose kingdom shall have no end." The poet is remembering his creed, whether Apostles' or Nicene, a part of the daily liturgy which he had known verbatim from childhood, and is fitting it most appropriately into its place in Michael's narrative: it is that part of the narrative for which there is no direct Biblical account, nothing more than sketchy mentions here and there; it is that part dealing with the future, not only for Adam but for the reader; it is that part requiring the most of the Christian's faith. Milton here follows the orthodox position, as he does in the *Christian Doctrine*, Book I, Ch. XXXIII. Accordingly, he quotes and elaborates the most familiar statement of that faith his readers could know. Liturgy has become source, and most appropriately, his last apparent quotation from liturgy and his last direct use of one in the poem is that part which looks to the future.

In a sense all the quotations and echoes from liturgy, all the religious rites and ceremonies suggested or presented in *Paradise Lost*, look toward the future. They from the first were present; they belong to Eden or earlier; from them emerge later and more elaborate forms, more express, precise, and prescribed forms. What became Matins, Evensong, the marriage ceremony, grace before meat, the Consecration

Form, and the Lord's Supper appear in their original and natural state. Yet what they are here is indicated by echoes from the future, by what they were to become: time past is not only present in time future, but finds its means of expression also in time future. Reconstructing the originals out of the patterns and meanings of what they had become, the poet recognizes form and uses it—but with the greatest of freedom. In this dawn of time forms and rites had not grown rigid. The Spirit that dove-like sat brooding over the vast abyss did make it pregnant, and the forms that rose out of Chaos were living forms. Adam's grace before dinner goes unrecognized as such by its very speaker—and by many a reader. The Children's Canticle is cut to fit the time and the occasion. The marriage grows so naturally out of the occasion that only the realization of its meaning makes it a ceremony. The sacrament before the high altar of God is offered by the first priest, the surrogate, himself the sacrifice to come. And we recognize the consecration of the cosmos to its Creator suddenly when we hear the angelic hosts break into the words of Psalm xxiv, from earliest times the proper opening for consecration of Christ's home. Built and consecrated, however, when He came into it, the world knew Him not. His manifestation to it involved the next rite, the first sacrament.

3

PARADISE REGAINED

$\mathcal{T}$HE SECONDARY title of *Paradise Regained* might have been *Ecce Homo*. If the Son came into the world and the world knew Him not, it is only fair to say, if we accept Milton's account, that He knew not Himself—not until after the baptism and the temptation. He had got inklings, of course, from inner promptings and his mother's words— the Annunciation and the *Magnificat, the Gloria in excelsis*, the *Nunc dimittis* of Simeon—but no public expression from on high or testings for proof on earth. The poem is a study in self-recognition and in manifestation; it is also the story of the Son's preparation for his teaching and his Passion—the ultimate act of salvation.[1] The first step in this recognition, manifestation, and preparation is the sacrament of Baptism. His is the first, the original Christian Baptism; and like the adumbration of the Lord's Supper in *Paradise Lost*, it involves the paradox of the Real Presence: in whose name is He baptized but His own?

We do not have in the Biblical accounts the actual words spoken by John Baptist at the immersion, nor does Milton furnish us with them. He is more interested, as were the four Evangelists, in the consecration spoken from Heaven following Jesus's going "up out of the water" and in the descent of the dove. With the meaning, not the words, he is concerned:

> on him baptiz'd
> Heaven open'd, and in likeness of a Dove
> The Spirit descended, while the Father's voice
> From Heav'n pronounc'd him his beloved Son. (I, 29-32)

By these words the Son is recognized and declared by the Father, and by the descent of the dove visible sign is given. All three persons of the Trinity are present, and hereafter men will be baptized in the name of the Three: the Father, the Son, and the Holy Ghost. It is the new baptism, the joining of the spirits of men with that of God, not merely the washing away of sins of John's baptism. By this baptism, according to the liturgy, the "Olde Adam" in man is to be so buried that the new man may be raised up in him; by it he becomes a child of God and an inheritor of the kingdom of Heaven, an adopted son of God (the meaning of which term Satan ponders); by it he is required to "fight under his [Christ's] banner against sinne, the world, and the deuyll, and to continue Christes faithful souldiour and servant vnto his liues ende." This fight is immediately joined between Satan and the Son following the Son's baptism, with Satan taking the offensive. The poet's handling is remarkably apposite, for this is the act of initiation. It is especially appropriate that the founder of the new faith become the instrument of the new covenant in His role as man, as yet not realizing His Godhead. He is Man's representative and, as Man, assumes the contest with Satan.

It is just as apposite that Milton, after very brief preliminaries,[2] uses the baptism as the initial scene of the poem. Out of it springs the entire action: Satan's speculations and his diabolic conclave in middle air, the parallel council in Heaven with the Father's explanations, and Jesus's withdrawal into the desert, the temptations there to follow. Just as the initiation of baptism is the beginning of Jesus's ministry, so it furnishes the poet the proper beginning for his work. Milton might have begun his poem on the temptation where Giles Fletcher began *Christ's Victory on Earth*, with the Son already alone in the desert protected from wild beasts by Mercy, but Milton's craftsmanship was better than Fletcher's. Ready at hand as a part of the story was a natural and a sacramental beginning, and the poet used it effectively as basic to his art and meaning.

The next ceremony occurs in Heaven following the formal statement of the Father to Michael that now the Son will as man be exposed to Satan's machinations and be tested before He may through humiliation and death earn man's salvation. The angels then sing their hymn, moving rhythmically around the throne:

> Victory and Triumph to the Son of God
> Now ent'ring his great duel, not of arms,
> But to vanquish by wisdom hellish wiles.
> The Father knows the Son; therefore secure
> Ventures his filial Virtue, though untried,
> Against whate'er may tempt, whate'er seduce,
> Allure, or terrify, or undermine. (I, 173-79)

The canticle here sung, like so many of the angelic anthems, reminds us of the descriptions of angelic worship in Revelation, such as those in Chapters xiv and xv. But it also draws upon i John v, 4: "For whatsoever is born of God overcometh the world: and this is the victory that overcometh the world, even our faith;" and upon the Gospel of John x, 15: "As the Father knoweth me, even so I know the Father." But more directly, I believe, he depends upon Psalm xcviii, the *Cantate Domino* of Evening Prayer cited above, for He will now get himself the victory. Milton, indeed, like the makers of such liturgical canticles before him as the *Gloria in excelsis*,[3] created his canticles out of remembered phrases, bits and scraps beautifully fused, of Scripture and earlier canticles, especially those he had heard so often. Nevertheless the *Cantate Domino* seems closest and especially appropriate. Just as it celebrates the redemptive acts of God, so Milton's angels sing the assurance of the redemptive act of the Son.

Appropriateness also marks the next instance of ceremonial, the complaint of the early apostles, "plain fishermen," who have just heard Jesus proclaimed Son of God, but now cannot find Him. Within the complaint they quote their earlier joyful outburst:

> Our eyes beheld
> Messiah certainly now come, so long
> Expected of our Fathers; we have heard
> His words, his wisdom full of grace and truth;
> Now, now, for sure, deliverance is at hand,
> The Kingdom to Israel shall be restored. (II, 31-36)

It is altogether proper that they quote the last words of the Gospel for Christmas Day, John i, 14: "full of grace and truth." In so doing they remind the reader of the entire prologue to the Fourth Gospel, itself derived from a Psalm, and the meaning of the Logos. The poet's concern for the meaning is emphasized none too subtly in the first part of the line, "His words, his wisdom," for not only was He called the Word, but the Word was called Wisdom. Milton deliberately inserts this quotation from their earlier song of joy into the Apostles' lament to emphasize again the theme of the poem or the question it involves: Who is this man? What is the meaning of the Incarnation? It is reemphasized by their "perplexity and new amaze," now He seems lost, for they believe Him to be the Messiah.

Following their questioning and wonderment at the seeming loss comes their petition, prefaced with the expression of their need which might well have been written by the Psalmist:

> God of *Israel*,
> Send thy Messiah forth, the time is come;
> Behold the Kings of th' Earth how they oppress
> Thy chosen, to what height thir pow'r unjust
> They have exalted, and behind them cast
> All fear of thee; arise and vindicate
> Thy Glory, free thy people from thir yoke! (II, 42-48)

Rhythms and diction, phrasing and syntax are from the Psalms or one of the prophets: "The kings of the earth set themselves, and the rulers take counsel together against the LORD, and against his anointed." (Psalm ii, 2) The echoes are too numerous to be listed. The lament and prayer of the early Apostles appropriately emerge out of their own psalms and prayers. Milton has fashioned the passage for them out of their proper Scriptures, as was the practice of the earlier makers of liturgy.

Mary's meditation that immediately follows the lament and deals with the same subject, though not in itself ceremony or ritual, nevertheless refers to or suggests parts of liturgy. She remembers Michael's *Ave Maria*, she refers to Simeon's prophecy immediately following his *Nunc dimittis*, and she echoes faintly her own *Magnificat*. In each of these references she is concerned with the irony or ambiguity of her position. Hailed as "highly favor'd, among women blest," she seems destined for sorrow; though she must remember how old Simeon rejoiced that "mine eyes have seen thy Salvation," she speaks only of his prophecy of trouble in Israel and "that through my very Soul/A sword shall pierce;" and remembering the exaltation of which she sang in the *Magnificat*, she speaks ironically of "My Exaltation to Afflictions high." She ends her meditation still puzzled, waiting "with thoughts / Meekly compos'd." Liturgical materials, the canticles of great joy, are deliberately questioned as they are alluded to or obliquely suggested; they are not said or sung. Milton is deliberately contrasting the joy they express at the Incarnation with the consequent sorrow and suffering. The somber forebodings of Mary's musings set the proper mood for the terrors of the temptation as well as for the ultimate sorrow when she stands before the cross. But she is inured to wait with patience; she will not distrust. If she has intimations of the cross, she has from the inspired canticles the right to hope for an empty tomb.

And at the very end of the poem the angelic choir turns hope into assurance. The anthem they sing, though in secret sung, asserts and celebrates the resolution, the denouement, the answer to the questioning of Satan, the Apostles, Mary, and the Son Himself. In it the promise indicated in the invocation is kept: that He shall be brought forth "By proof th'undoubted Son of God." With table spread before Him and celestial food, symbolizing the Lord's Supper,[4] the angels sing thus in part:

> True Image of the Father, whether thron'd
> In the bosom of bliss, and light of light
> Conceiving, or remote from Heaven, and enshrin'd
> In fleshly Tabernacle, and human form,
> Wand'ring the Wilderness, whatever place,
> Habit, or state, or motion, still expressing
> The Son of God, with Godlike force endu'd
> Against th' Attempter of thy Father's Throne,
> And thief of Paradise . . . (IV, 596-604)

This anthem, like that sung in Heaven to celebrate the Creation, celebrates the Son's great accomplishment. Unlike that sung in Heaven, the accomplishment is proof of his identity. Assertions of that identity are frequent in liturgy, but especially in the Creed. As one might expect, Milton here echoes the creeds. He could hardly escape doing so, for his mind was concerned with their substance, especially that of the Nicene Creed, as the pertinent part indicates:

And [I believe] in one Lord Jesus Christ, the only-begotten Son of God; Begotten of his Father before all worlds, God of God, Light of Light, Very God of Very God; Begotten, not made; Being of one substance with the Father; By whom all things were made: Who for us men and for our salvation came down from heaven, And was incarnate by the Holy Ghost of the Virgin Mary, and was made man. . . .

It might be argued that, as Milton the young man had written the Nativity Ode to celebrate the Incarnation, so Milton the mature poet wrote *Paradise Regained* to prove it, and the summary of the proof comes in the anthem of the angels. Like a proper canticle of praise, it opens with an acclamation, an assertion of the Godhead of the Son, the meaning if not the words best known from the Nicene Creed: "Image of the Father," "light of light conceiving," "enshrined in fleshly tabernacle," "Son of God."[5] The opening suggests in its imagery likewise the *Gloria in excelsis,* as might be expected. Following the acclamation of the opening, the angels recite the achievement of the exercise in the wilderness, and Milton draws upon numerous Biblical passages to be shaped into his own piece of liturgy, expecially from Psalm cxxiv, from Luke x, 18, and Malachi iv, 3, from Revelation ix, 11, and Job xxvi, 6, xxviii, 22. His practice is that of the writers of liturgy from earliest times.

The rituals and liturgical sections serve *Paradise Regained* structurally. The baptism serves as protasis, the chorus in heaven gives assurance of the outcome of the battle now joined, the ponderings of the Apostles and the meditations of Mary furnish dramatic irony in that the reader has better assurance than they of the outcome, and the final chorus asserts the denouement. Considered as a whole, the poem follows no pattern of church ritual; it provides no confession, absolution, sacrifice, or final blessing to enable the purified man to face the world, the flesh, and the devil. It does not need to, for the perfect man is already purified. He needs only to discover that He is the Son.

4

SAMSON AGONISTES

*U*NLIKE *Paradise Regained, Samson Agonistes* contains
no perfect man who needs only to discover his true nature.
Although it, too, involves self-discovery, Samson's life on his
last day follows something approaching a rite generally
analogous to a Christian liturgy. It moves from the agony
of despair to acknowledgment and confession of sin, from
confession through the tests of the temptations (interpola-
tions which might be considered as penance) to wisdom and
absolution, and from these to the moving of the Holy Spirit
which leads to the final sacrifice and salvation. The play
deals with the theme of regeneration, and the pattern of the

basic Christian rites provides for individual regeneration. Having patiently subdued the Old Adam in oneself and brought oneself to confession and repentance, having thus cleansed "the stony from" one's heart, one is ready to make "new flesh / Regenerate to grow instead," to strengthen one's faith by instruction so as to be able to follow the guidance of the Spirit toward the duties or sacrifices ahead. Perhaps the pattern is not too different from the four steps of Samson's regeneration as outlined by Professor Parker—the achievement of patience, of faith, of strength against the weakness of his sin, and the ability to recognize and obey the call to further service.[1]

Now, I do not wish to be misunderstood: *Samson Agonistes*, as all readers know, follows the form of Greek tragedy and is designed to accomplish the catharsis of Greek tragedy, as Milton tells us, but he also tells us that St. Paul and fathers of the Church had quoted, approved, and written such plays. Modern Italian Christian dramatists had effectively adapted the form to their use, especially the device of the chorus. Furthermore, the protagonist of his play was a Hebrew prototype of Christ. The story is Hebrew, the form is Greek, and the doctrine is Christian. He recognized in the form a kinship with Christian tradition or sufficient analogy with Christian ritual to warrant effective adaptation. He could not have failed to see the analogy between the Samson story and his plans for the Adam story as he had outlined it in the Cambridge Manuscript for a play. Doubtless, he recognized in Samson's soul-struggle the *psychomachia* of the morality play, the pattern of which so patently follows the plan of salvation and illustrates the basic plan of the basic services of the church, of whatever branch. In many ways it resembles the liturgical pattern of the last three books of *Paradise Lost*, as outlined above. A few details will show that the poet kept the basic pattern in mind, though he pushes the limits of form far beyond what any liturgist of earlier times or of his own reforming day would have done.

Perhaps the first suggestion that the action may involve

the healing and consolation of religious service is the statement by the Chorus in the opening of the first episode of its
purpose in visiting Samson. It has come

> To visit or bewail thee, or if better,
> Counsel or Consolation we may bring,
> Salve to thy Sores; apt words have power to swage
> The tumors of a troubl'd mind,
> And are as Balm to fester'd wounds. (ll. 182-86)

Their words suggest, if they do not invite, confession. Samson's following speech is an informal and bitter admission of
his betrayal of God through a woman's betrayal of himself.
It is also a bitter complaint about Israel's deserting him in his
leadership against the Philistines and about God's seeming
desertion of him. He is perplexed, impatient, disillusioned,
and in despair. The Chorus in reply to his state begins its
first stasimon, a sort of canticle echoing Revelation xv and
Psalms xiv and viii, in which it asserts the justice of God's
ways, although at times those ways may be hidden from
human reason. One's faith must not be shaken, even though
God breaks or seems to break His own laws. To achieve such
trust is basic to making one's own will conform to God's will,
and such conformity is the purpose of the religious service—
as well as the achievement of salvation through doing God's
will. The first step toward this conformity is confession,
acknowledgment of disobedience to God's will and acceptance of responsibility for our own wilful acts. Roused by
his father's questioning of God's justice and by his assertion
that Samson's failure has disgraced God before Dagon, he
makes such confession in the next episode, and he makes it
according to proper formulary. He begins with the beginning
words of almost all liturgical confessions, or with a paraphrase
of them:

> Father, I do acknowledge and confess
> That I this honor, I this pomp have brought
> To *Dagon*, and advanc'd his praises high
> Among the Heathen round; to God have brought
> Dishonor, obloquy, and op't the mouths

57

Of Idolists, and Atheists; have brought scandal
To *Israel*, diffidence of God, and doubt
In feeble hearts, propense enough before
To waver, or fall off and join with Idols:
Which is my chief affliction, shame and sorrow,
The anguish of my Soul, that suffers not
Mine eye to harbor sleep, or thoughts to rest.
This only hope relieves me, that the strife
With mee hath end. . . . (ll. 448-61)

The confessional part of the speech breaks off in the expression of the hope and assurance of God's triumph. The point is here that confessions regularly begin with "I do acknowledge and confess," or a variant of the formula. For example, even in John Knox's Book of Common Order "A Confession of all Estates and Times" begins: "O eternal God and most merciful Father, we confess and acknowledge here before thy divine majesty that we are miserable sinners. . . ."[2] Quite as important, Samson's confession to his father follows the general structure of confessions, in that it comes to a turning, a "but" or "on the other hand" or "now therefore," or "yet," or some such construction either expressed or implied. Samson's turn begins with "This only hope relieves me." He might have used a connective: "Yet this one hope." In the familiar General Confession of Morning and Evening Prayer, the turn comes with "but thou, O Lord, have mercy upon us." In the Prayer of Humble Access, a confession placed variously in the Anglican Communion Service at various times, the turn begins with "but thou art the same Lord whose property is always to have mercy." Just as Milton cues Eve's confession to Adam out of the *Confiteor*, so he cues Samson's more public confession out of the General Confession of the Communion Service of the Anglican liturgy, or out of any one of the many earlier liturgical confessions.

Mere confession is not enough to relieve Samson, however. His later speeches bewail his manifold sins and wickedness which have brought him to such condition as Mankind came in his morality play, to despair and prayer for death.

Although he has implored God's pardon, he believes his sins too great to expect God's mercy, except the mercy of death. Before the Chorus he repeats his feelings:

> Nor am I in the list of them that hope;
> Hopeless are all my evils, all remediless;
> This one prayer yet remains, might I be heard,
> No long petition, speedy death,
> The close of all my miseries and the balm. (ll. 647-51)

Here at the end of the protasis of the play the protagonist seemingly has come to the point of no return, to the unpardonable sin of despair; yet this expression, this very "sense of Heav'n's desertion," provides for the expression of God's greatest mercy. Even though He may, ironically as some have said,[8] grant His Champion's petition for death, in His great compassion He may also grant the fulfillment of his Champion's mission. Samson's despair derives not from pride as did that of Marlowe's Faustus or Shakespeare's Claudius, but from his feeling of failure and unworthiness, actually from his humility. He regards himself as alone responsible for God's desertion. He is willing to do God's will, but he despairs of God's trusting him with that power again. In fact, he does not trust himself. Having followed too much and too long the devices and desires of his own heart, he sees no reason why God should think he might change his ways and follow God's plans and desires. He can find no reason why God should put any further confidence in him. God's justice requires no such remission. Yet he does not deny God's mercy. Paradoxically, his hope for death is a hope for God's mercy, for release from further penance. He is utterly sorry for his misdeeds, and he has achieved humility. But, as the Absolution says, God desires not the death of a sinner; He pardons and absolves those truly penitent. Humility, however bitter, is the beginning of trust, and trust is the beginning of hope and regeneration. And basic liturgy provides the pattern: after confession and contrition new flesh regenerate is made to grow through instruction and the exercise of praise. So strength is increased until the Christian may be ready to go out and accomplish his mission. The very acknowledgement of his helplessness and the hopelessness of his evils is the beginning of Samson's reassurance.

At this point, then, the Chorus of stasimon 2 can counsel patience and hope. Even though in His inscrutable way God may seem to desert his elect and to favor the "common rout," He must be trusted still. Near the end of this stasimon the Chorus can pray God to restore Samson to his labors, his mission. The prayer involves absolution, for restoration requires penitence: penitent and cleansed by God's mercy, Samson may now be given another chance. The liturgical character of this chorus becomes more apparent when one observes that it is fashioned largely out of Scripture —out of Psalms xxxvii and viii, Hebrews i, Ecclesiastes vii, Job vii, and perhaps other passages unrecognized—the same liturgical materials out of which earlier and contemporary liturgies were formed.

At this point Samson is weakest; there is no health in him. He must be strengthened. To be strengthened he must regain faith in himself, but paradoxically self-confidence can come only through strengthening his faith, his trust in God. The testings which follow—the episodes of Dalila, Harapha, and the Officer—provide the means for the strengthening. They are instructive, as if lessons in a liturgy. Alternately with them come the stasima, choruses which serve as comment and interpretation of the lessons to be drawn from the episodes and as canticles of praise. These episodes and stasima serve a purpose somewhat like that served by the visions and narrative which Michael presents to Adam in *Paradise Lost*. They can be thought of as roughly analogous to the sections of Morning and Evening Prayer of instruction and praise following the Absolution and leading to the affirmation of the Creed. For example, the Chorus following the Dalila episode summarizes the lesson to be learnt from it—the lesson about women which Samson has finally learned and proved. Much the same is true of the next episode and chorus. Samson learns to overcome his pride in his own strength and to trust God to provide him in his need: "My trust is in the living God." The indignities he suffers

> I deserve and more,
> Acknowledge them from God inflicted on me
> Justly, yet despair not of his final pardon
> Whose ear is ever open.   (ll. 1169-72)

Not despairing now, he can challenge Harapha to combat and stand him down. The chorus, stasimon 4, which follows celebrates the return of Samson's strength. A canticle of praise, it is full of Scriptural echoes such as that from Isaiah lvii, Ephesians vi, and Revelation xiv. The final episode brings with it the peripeteia: Samson has gained such courage as to trust "Some rousing motions in me." His will has now become God's will. It is an affirmation of utter belief. The chorus which follows is a benediction:

> Go, and the Holy One
> Of *Israel* be thy guide
> To what may serve his glory best, and spread his name
> Great among the Heathen round. (ll. 1427-30)

It is also a proper call for action for the Christian soldier, now properly equipped in the full armor of God. It echoes both the familiar *"Ite"* of the *"Ite Missa est"* of the Mass and Psalm lxxxix, Judges xiii and perhaps Malachi i and other Biblical passages. Like Spenser's Red Cross, Samson is ready now for the contest. The poet seems consciously aware of liturgical implications and values—the service, the ritual, is preparation.

Here the analogy between the poem and the basic services of Morning and Evening Prayer and the Lord's Supper fairly well ends, though the exodus and the conclusion show some slight resemblance to the intercessions following the commitment of the Creed.[4] The kommos and part of the last speech of Manoa suggest another sort of service. They suggest a requiem, and the last lines of the poem surely echo the *Nunc dimittis*.[5] The assurance Manoa gives us, that "which is best and happiest yet, all this / With God not parted from him, as was fear'd," is wrought out of the prayer at the opening of the Service of the Burial of the Dead "suffer vs not at our last houre for any paines of death to fall from the." And the consolation of the final chorus, "All is best, though we oft," I submit, is closer in doctrine to this same Christian ritual than it is to the formulary out of Greek drama on which it is patterned and to which the critics so often call our attention. It bears also the mark of the Christian formulary. Essentially, it asserts the highest trust in God and His Providence, suggesting Job's words as one finds them in the Burial Service: "The Lord geueth, and the Lorde taketh awaye. Euen as it hath pleased the Lorde so commeth thynges to passe: Blessed be the name of the Lorde."

What is perhaps of more importance concerning the ritualistic qualities of *Samson Agonistes* lies in the reaffirmation of the covenant. God did not desert Samson. Although he seemed to have done so, on the last day he reaffirmed his covenant with his champion. The play is really concerned with this whole matter. As we have seen, Milton considered a sacrament as a reaffirmation of God's covenant with man. Basically the play becomes sacrament, especially if we further consider Samson as "a reasonable, holy and liuely sacrifice," who has offered himself for his people and has kept his covenant through this ritual.

In *Samson Agonistes* Milton obviously follows the form of the Greek tragedy, though with considerable modification; not so obviously, he bends to his need something out of basic liturgy and ritual. He has not here forgotten what he had learned from the morality play in his plans for *Paradise Lost*, nor was he oblivious of the ritual and liturgy he knew. He seems to have been consciously suggesting it and also creating it out of the same materials that his predecessors and contemporaries used. Earlier liturgies and the Scriptures furnished substance and form for his literary production, though he may obscure the form and force it to its outer limits.

62

CONCLUSION

$\mathcal{N}$O ONE will maintain that Milton was a writer of formal liturgies or a builder of rites and ceremonies for church use. His larger forms are basically secular, deriving from classical and Renaissance genres. Even with them he varies his patterns from the orthodox: he would be master of form, not its servant. Furthermore, he often expressed his scorn for rites and liturgies as becoming outworn and incapable of expressing the true and immediate thoughts and feelings of their speakers. They tend to become mere form without substance. Yet the occasions for rites and ceremony exist repeatedly. They spring unpremeditated out of human affairs, and their expression should be as spontaneous as their occurrence. Grace before meat should come as Adam's came, out of the natural goodness of the man. But the occasion for the expression of this grace comes frequently; and it should be as frequently observed, though not necessarily expressed in the same words. The same is true of other occasions for formal expressions. A rite becomes necessary merely because the occasion is repeated; but it must be kept simple, sincere, and natural, and its words must be chosen for the immediate occasion. Of course, the length of any such rite is restricted by the length of the poem. Except for the suggestion of liturgical pattern in the poem as a whole, it often can only be suggested. The poet depends frequently upon cues, allusions in the form of tags from ceremony or ritual, to guide the reader and enable him to recognize some of the less obvious meanings and overtones of the poetry.

In looking back over these references or allusions and the more obvious uses of ritual in the poems as well, one finds a surprising number of rites and ceremonies: aside from grace before the meal, if I am not badly misled, we have an Asperges, marriage, morning and evening prayers, the Lord's Supper, Baptism, and the rite of consecration of a church. In addition to these suggestions of rather complete rites, the poems contain confessions, echoes from various prayers of the Book of Common Prayer, several "Ave's," repeated echoes of the *Gloria in excelsis* and other canticles, *requiescats*, reference to the "Comfortable Words" of the Lord's Supper, and echoes from the creeds, benedictions, and from the Thanksgiving of the Lord's Supper. This does not mean, of course, that Milton did not know the Scriptural origins of all these, but more likely he conveniently recognized their use in the rites and liturgies of the Church and by so doing marked them as such in his poetry.

Remarkable as the number of these may seem, their function is more important. The Nativity Ode, *Paradise Lost*, and *Paradise Regained*, for example, take their initial impulses from prayer or rites: the poet-priest's prayer for pure lips, the preacher's prayer for illumination, and the baptism out of which subsequent action comes. A turning point or the denouement of *Comus, Lycidas, Paradise Lost*, and *Samson Agonistes* is also effected through rites or ceremonies or is involved in them: the rites of Comus and the Asperges of

Sabrina in the first, the burial service in *Lycidas,* the Lord's Supper in *Paradise Lost,* the Creed in the angels' anthem in *Paradise Regained,* and the benediction, especially in *Samson Agonistes.* Coming as these do at critical points, these reflections of rites and ceremony seem to have been chosen deliberately as a means for heightening the action and deepening the meaning. Ceremonial and ritual in fiction as in life dramatizes and celebrates occasion. Adam and Eve's confession and repentance, the turning point in their lives whereby they made possible the redemption of the race, is rightfully celebrated in the sacrament which follows.

The clarification or extension of meanings implied by the recognized rituals or suggested by echoes from liturgy are perhaps even more valuable to understanding and appreciation. The simple recognition of the *pax vobiscum* of the elegies and the monodies provides an extension of value, if it does not add another dimension to the meaning. The recognition of the phrase from the Gospel for Christmas Day in the Apostles' lament and its appropriateness in *Paradise Regained* illuminates the passage. The brilliant use of "Daystar" with its *double entendre* in *Lycidas* recognized from liturgy, or the equally brilliant use of the Real Presence in the adumbration of the Eucharist and in the institution of Christian Baptism compounds the meaning and intensifies it almost beyond expression. The recognition of Samson's confession as formalized by the liturgical words or his benediction sung by the Chorus as a dismissal suggesting the last words of the Mass lend a significance beyond the literal statement. These are but a few instances of the enrichment of Milton's poetry out of religious rites and ceremonies.

Furthermore, I am certain that Milton felt, especially in *Paradise Lost* and *Paradise Regained,* an obligation to give an account of how rites and ceremonies, special prayers and liturgies, got started. He tries to show how they sprang naturally into being as institutions among men and were established for later generations to be guided by—not slavishly and meaninglessly repeated. The occasion may be much the same as it recurs, but the words for its celebration need not be the same. Each new celebration, indeed, should in its freshness of expression be as nearly like the first as possible; its expression should spring anew, so that it will be true expression, genuine and sincere: "The meaning, not the Name I call." Yet in putting the rites and liturgies into his poems, Milton followed, if quite distantly, his predecessors and contemporaries among liturgists. Like them, he draws upon earlier liturgies and upon the Scriptures. Especially in the composition of his anthems for the angels, he draws upon the Psalms as well as the canticles of the Church liturgy, and he is careful to draw upon those already recognized as especially appropriate for any specific occasion.

In so doing he sets off the occasion as having special value. Indeed, it has the effect of elevating and dramatizing the repeated celebration. This special recognition tends to universalize: as often as the occasion presents itself, it shall be recognized and memorialized in the same general manner and given the same general formulary, spontaneity being required. By all men it should be so memorialized and celebrated. In this way they recognize their common humanity and their common relationship to God. More important, such celebration, such ceremony and ritual, following Milton's understanding of the meaning of sacrament, reaffirms man's covenant with God. The reaffirmation of the covenant is an acceptance of God's will and a reassertion of trust in His Providence. Throughout Milton's poetry and central to the conflict in much of it is the temptation to distrust God and to rebel against His will. Given freedom of will, paradoxically, man truly achieves this freedom only when he makes it conform to God's will. The rebellious cry in *Lycidas* or the question in the Sonnet 19, On His Blindness, Eve's trust in the serpent, Adam's overt disobedience, Samson's *hybris*, and the Son's temptations in the wilderness are all central to the conflicts of the poems in which they occur. All are resolved by a reaffirmation of trust and obedience, which forms the very basis of Christian ritual and liturgy. Whether or not

Milton was deliberately remembering and reflecting the Prayer Book, his theme was its most constant theme: Out of the Lord's Prayer "Thy will be done on earth as it is heaven" and out of the Collect for Peace in both Morning and Evening Prayer, "whose service is perfect freedom." Called to his attention, I am reasonably sure he would have recognized the similarity, if not identity, of his purpose to that of Christian ritual.

I am also reasonably certain Milton recognized a similarity between the style and structure of some of his poems and the basic structure of much familiar liturgy. Whether or not he did, in his epics especially he achieves a high ritual. C. S. Lewis in his discussion of the style of the Secondary epic, the category into which he would place *Paradise Lost*, observes that it requires a higher solemnity than the Primary (Homeric) epic, but that it has lost the external aids the Primary enjoyed:

> There is no robed and garlanded *aoidos*, no altar, not even a feast hall—only a private person reading a book in an armchair. Yet somehow or other, that private person must be made to feel that he is assisting in august ritual, for if he does not, he will not be receptive of the true epic exhilaration. . . . Every judgment on it which does not realize this will be inept. To blame it [*Paradise Lost*] for being ritualistic or incantatory, for lacking intimacy or the speaking voice, is to blame it for being just what it intends to be and ought to be.[1]

I have been concerned throughout this study with making explicit this very point. Milton's actual use of religious ritual and ceremony takes us beyond style and into structure itself. *Paradise Lost* was first thought of as a sort of morality play or *sacre rappresentazione*, and the morality play, after the protasis, follows basic liturgical form—confession, repentance, absolution, instruction and praise, prayers, and then the facing of death—or the world. More than a suggestion of this arrangement is evident, as we have observed, in *Comus* and *Lycidas*, as well as in *Paradise Lost* and *Samson Agonistes*.

Here again, however, the poet is no slave to form. Rather he keeps it in the background, unobtrusive and organic. His achievement of freedom within form must, then, be extended to his quiet employment of religious rite and ceremony in his poetry. And the recognition of these forms, though they are kept subordinate, is a recognition of an elevation and a richness in Milton's poetry hitherto largely unrecognized, or at least unregarded.

NOTES

INTRODUCTION

[1] "Milton," reprinted from *The Proceedings of the British Academy*, XXXIII (1948), 19.

[2] Arthur Barker, "Structural Pattern in *Paradise Lost*," *Philological Quarterly*, XXVIII (Jan., 1949), 17.

[3] Among numerous expressions of his opposition is his complaint in *Eikonoklastes* against the Book of Common Prayer, which is little more than "the old Mass-Book don into English" and in which he denounces liturgy because it "confines by force" and imprisons prayer (*Works*, V, 220-21); or against ceremony in *The Reason of Church Government Urged Against Prelaty*, in which he maintains that actions must be grounded in nature and not in ceremony (*Works*, III, 197-98); or in the *Christian Doctrine* in which he objects to Christians taking over certain rites from heathen and Jew and for using "the external forms but without any accompanying affection of the mind." (*Works*, XV, 75-77). Yet he admits in the *Christian Doctrine* the institution of the two sacraments of Baptism and the Lord's Supper and has no objection to the other Christian rites such as Confirmation, Penance, Orders, and Unction. But he would disallow marriage as a purely religious rite. In all of these, however, whether called sacraments or not—and he is concerned with "The meaning, not the Name"—he objects that the two first should be regarded as necessary to salvation or any of them being thought of as other than a solemn sign or symbol. He would disallow infant baptism; yet he would require immersion

in the performance of the sacrament (See *Works*, XVI, 165-71.) Milton's concern is that rites and ceremonies may, through thoughtless repetition and outworn custom, corrupt the world. As I deal with individual cases in the poetry, I shall refer more particularly to Milton's direct comments about various rituals. My references to the prose are to *The Works of John Milton*, ed. Frank Allen Patterson and others, 18 vols. (New York, 1931-1942).

[4] D. L. Clark, *Milton at St. Paul's School* (New York, 1948), 110, gives an account of the daily routine at St. Paul's school; and David Masson, *The Life of John Milton* (London, 1881), I, 136-37, gives the routine for the Cambridge student. He tells us that the bell rang at five o'clock in the morning, assembling the students at chapel "to hear the morning-service of the Church," and that they were required to attend "evening-service in the Chapel." Ernest Brennecke, Jr., *John Milton the Elder and His Music*, Columbia University Studies in Musicology, No. 2 (New York, 1938), gives a thorough account of the elder Milton's musical composition. He quotes his Latin motet, the words of which the elder Milton had originally sung as a choir boy at Compline. (p. 84) John Milton, Sr., also set the majestic opening sentences of The Order for the Buriall of the Dead from the Elizabethan version of The Book of Common Prayer: "I am the resurrection and the life, saithe the Lord." (p. 85) Except for such familiar parts as the creeds, my quotations are taken from *The Prayer-Book of Queen Elizabeth, 1559* (London, 1890).

[5] See William B. Hunter, Jr., "Milton Translates the Psalms," *Philological Quarterly*, XL (1961), 485-94, for full treatment of Milton's use of contemporary paraphrases of the psalms.

1. THE MINOR POEMS

[1] It should be noted here that before a Catholic priest reads the Gospel at Mass, he prays that his heart and lips may be cleansed as God cleansed the lips of Isaiah "with the burning coal." See also footnote 21 below. Rosemond Tuve has noted that the Hymn is itself a liturgical piece "presented" as if an offertory; she also observes that the reference to Leviathan belongs to a lesson for Matins on December 7 (Isaiah xxvii) and was combined with Psalm lxxxix to form the offertory for Christmas Day. See her *Images & Themes in Five Poems by Milton* (Cambridge, Mass., 1957), 52, 63.

² In stanza VI the speaker is transported to Salem, where his soul in holy vision sits. My references to the poems are to *John Milton's Complete Poems and Major Prose*, ed. Merritt Y. Hughes (New York, 1957), hereafter cited as Hughes.

³ Hardly a religious affair, the poet's *At a Vacation Exercise* was written for a ceremony. It is perhaps worth noticing that his *In Obituum Procancellarii Medici* ends with a *requiescat*, and *Elegia Tertia*, on the death of Bishop Lancelot Andrewes, closes its vision with an echo of Matthew xxv: 21, "Nate, veni, et patrii felix cape gaudia regni: / Semper ab hinc duro, nate, labore vaca," another *requiescat*. *Elegia Septima*, about Venus and Cupid, a poem with "perverse spirit and trifling purpose," ends with a playful prayer to Cupid. *L'Allegro* and *Il Penseroso* each begins with an exorcism, and reflections of other ceremonials or rituals appear in others of the shorter poems, such as those in the Hobson poems and the *requiescat* in *An Epitaph on the Marchioness of Winchester* (ll. 47-48).

⁴ See *The Reason for Church Government Urged against Prelaty* (*Works*, III, 247-48) and *Christian Doctrine* (*Works*, XVI, 165).

⁵ See *The Faithful Shepherdess*, I. i. 138-57. Here the Priest enters and, sprinkling the shepherds with water, begins with these words:

> Shepherds, thus I purge away
> Whatsoever this great day
> Or the past hours gave not good
> To corrupt your maiden blood.

He ends his speech with an *Ite*: "Go your ways; ye are all clear." This Asperges seems to me better to illustrate Milton's indebtedness to Fletcher's play than the passage commonly cited, wherein Amarillis heals Amoret with water from the well, III. i. 378 ff. I quote from the edition of this play in *Elizabethan and Stuart Plays*, ed. Baskervill, Heltzel, and Nethercot (New York, 1934).

⁶ Actually two rites are combined in each case. In the first the invocation of Cotytto with the dance is followed by the enchantment of the victim, though the enchantment is implied, not expressed. The invocation of Sabrina is combined with her rite of purification which frees the Lady.

Northrop Frye thinks the action of *Comus* "moves up to the sprinkling of the Lady by Sabrina, an act with some analogies to baptism". (See "The Typology of *Paradise Regained*" *Modern Philology*, LIII [1956], 230). He makes this observation after having read, somewhat erroneously, A.S.P. Woodhouse's article

"Comus Once More", *University of Toronto Quarterly*, XIX (1950), 221-22.

⁷ See, for example, Northrop Frye, "Literature as Context: Milton's *Lycidas*," in *Milton's Lycidas: The Tradition and the Poem*, ed. C. A. Patrides (New York, 1961), 200-201.

⁸ Don Cameron Allen has shown that the pagan consolations for the dead were adapted by Christian rhetoricians for the comfort of the mourners at a funeral. Gregory Nazianzen (whose work Milton knew), for example, sets up a very model for the Christian funeral oration in his memorial sermon for his brother Caesar. See "The Translation of the Myth," in Allen's *The Harmonious Vision: Studies in Milton's Poetry* (Baltimore, 1956), 44-47.

⁹ Though sermons varied from preacher to preacher, an account of the virtuous life of the deceased was generally given and his salvation presented as a consolation and hope for the hearers. Donne, for example, in his funeral sermon for Sir William Cokayne considers at length Martha's imperfect faith in her outcry to Christ: "Lord, if thou hadst been here, my brother had not died," using it to exemplify the general imperfection of man's faith, the impermanence of temporal things, and the weakness of man's best actions—weakness in faith, hope, and charity. Then he spends the last section of his sermon as a memorial to Cokayne, whose life furnishes consolation for all men. Similarly, Donne's memorial sermon for Lady Danvers instructs the living and commemorates the dead; and the Lady's life has become an example for all who may come after her. She has achieved the peace of heaven in the embrace of Christ. Another excellent example is the sermon preached by the Bishop of Ely at the burial of Lancelot Andrewes, Bishop of Winchester. He develops the text "To do good and to distribute forget not; for with such sacrifices God is well pleased" throughout the first half of the sermon. Throughout the second half he uses the character of Andrewes as an example of the proper fulfilment of the text, the *applicatio* of the text, and a consolation. This sermon is included among the *Ninety-Six Sermons* of Lancelot Andrewes, 5 vols., Library of Anglo-Catholic Theology (Oxford, 1874), V, 265-306.

¹⁰ See Andrewes, *Sermons*, V, 305.

¹¹ Aside from the consolation at the end of the *Epitaphium Damonis*, little in that poem suggests religious ritual or even a memorial service such as one observes in *Lycidas*. The framework is given at the beginning: an outside "persona" tells the story of how the shepherd-poet, returning from abroad, realizes after

some time his great loss in the death of his friend and former companion; he sits under his favorite elm and recites a lament for the loss, remembering his absence abroad and speaking of his plans for a British epic. No procession of mourners appears, though the shepherd remembers that his friends have comforted him in his loss. At the end he consoles himself that Damon, pure and chaste, and now among the souls of heroes and the immortal gods "Aethereos haurit latices et gaudia potat / Ore Sacro." But no echoes from the burial ritual occurs. It should be noted that Sonnet 14 "On the Religious Memory of Mrs. Catharine Thomason" tells us that Love and Faith led on and furnished wings so that the Lady's good deeds could appear before Heaven's Judge, who gave her rest and drink from the streams of heaven. It suggests the *requiescat*. Although Macaulay thought Sonnet 18 "On the Late Massacre in Piedmont," as well as others among Milton's sonnets, resembles the collects of the Prayer Book, I do not find such likeness. It is a prayer for vengeance and, as such, a piece of liturgy. It comes near to being a curse or a Protestant anathema.

2. PARADISE LOST

[1] See *Coleridge's Miscellaneous Criticism*, ed. T. M. Raysor (Cambridge, Mass., 1936), 161.

[2] See Miss Carpenter's "Music in the *Secundum Pastorum*," *Speculum*, XXVI (1951), 696-700.

[3] This basic liturgical pattern may be recognized most easily in Morning Prayer and Evening Prayer in the Book of Common Prayer. It is present in the sacrament of the Lord's Supper, though much complicated by its retention of the ancient Mass of the Catechumens as a sort of ante-Mass.

[4] Later when I discuss the particular rites as they are suggested in certain parts of the poem, I hope to show that at the very center of Adam and Eve's redemption is Milton's original of the Lord's Supper.

[5] The prayer is spoken *sotto voce*: "cleanse my heart and my lips, Almighty God, as you cleansed the lips of the prophet Isaiah with the burning coal. In your mercy so cleanse me that I may worthily proclaim your holy gospel. Bless me, O Lord. The Lord be in my heart and on my lips that I may worthily and fittingly proclaim his Gospel." The priest then crosses his forehead, his lips, and his breast.

Helen Gardner has called attention to the change of style

in the second part of the exordium of the poem and has pointed out that it is a Christian prayer. For a fuller discussion, see her *A Reading of Paradise Lost* (Oxford, 1965), 16-20.

6 See J. W. Blench, *Preaching in England in the Late Fifteenth and Sixteenth Centuries: A Study of English Sermons 1450–c, 1600* (New York, 1964), 72, 103-104. The vast majority of Elizabethan preachers, after reading the sacred Scripture (their text), pronounced an invocation (sometimes said a bidding prayer and recited with the congregation the Lord's Prayer), spoke an exordium, set forth a proposition and the divisions, presented a confirmation and a confutation, and then made a conclusion, usually in the form of an *applicatio*, an urging to action.

7 See William Haller, *The Rise of Puritanism* (New York, 1938), 317-23, for a discussion of *Comus* and *Lycidas* as sermons or testimony of Milton's "effectual calling from God." Professor Haller does not consider the forms of the poems; rather their preaching. He believes that Milton's great poem, *Paradise Lost*, was the poet's justification for abandoning the pulpit.

8 In his introduction to *Paradise Lost*, Merritt Y. Hughes summarizes the various opinions as to the identity of this spirit who dovelike sat brooding on the vast abyss. He concludes that "the mystery of his Muse is incrutable." See his *John Milton: Complete Poems and Major Prose*, 198-99.

9 See his article, "The Hymn 'Veni Creator Spiritus,'" *American Ecclesiastical Review*, VI (June, 1897), 573-96, for discussion of the date, provenance, authorship, history, meaning, and text of the hymn. I quote from Henry's text. A translation of it appeared in the two versions of the Prayer Book of Edward VI and has been retained in the Anglican rite.

10 Helen Gardner notices that Milton's account of the natural wedding of Adam and Eve actually embodies the explanation of the purpose of marriage as added to the Sarum Rite in the First Prayer Book of Edward VI and retained in the Book of Common Prayer: namely, that it " 'is ordained of God in the time of man's innocency.' " See her *A Reading of Paradise Lost* (Oxford, 1965), 86.

11 See Hughes, *Poems and Prose*, 295, n. 724-35.

12 See *The Student's Milton*, ed. Frank Allen Patterson (New York, 1936), p. 84 of the "Notes." More frequently, as in Hughes, 306, Psalm cxlviii is said to parallel the hymn, and the Canticle is ignored. But both the Canticle and Adam's and Eve's hymn are much more extensive than this Psalm; in the hymn are at least eighteen images identical with images in the

74

Canticle, but only eleven identical with those of the Psalm and every one of those in the Psalm will be found in the Canticle; and whereas Psalm cxlviii has no *dramatis personae*, the Canticle, like *Paradise Lost*, does have: the three Children of Men who sang in the fiery furnace. Milton, of course, knew the Psalm, but he had probably heard the Canticle sung a thousand times, and its magnificent imagery came to him unpremeditated as he wrote. The Canticle is itself expanded from the Psalm. See Massey H. Shepherd, *The Oxford American Prayer Book Commentary* (Oxford, 1950), 13.

[13] See his *The Muse's Method: An Introduction to "Paradise Lost"* (Cambridge, Mass., 1962), 71-86. Professor Summers observes that "The hymn is the poem's chief exemplum of the perfect human hymn of praise by unfallen man; as such it mirrors in little the larger structure." He suggests the movement from the abstract to the larger concrete images, to the more particular, and he divides up the hymn into strophes based upon these steps in the movement. He notes that the commentators refer to the Psalms, particularly Psalm cxlviii, as the source for the passage; he fails to note that it comes more directly from the Canticle of the Children, which actually lends it its form and helps make it a great hymn of praise.

[14] *The Primer Set Fvrth By the Kinges Maiestie & his Clergie, to be taught lerned, and red: & none other to be vsed throrwout all his Dominions* (London: Printed by Richard Grafton, 1546), A3r-v.

[15] *The Works of John Knox*, ed. David Laing, 6 vols. (Edinburgh, 1895), VI, 348.

[16] *The Early Works of Thomas Becon*, ed. John Ayre, Parker Society (Cambridge, 1843), II, 26. This same grace is still retained in the Roman Missal in The Prayer Before Dinner.

[17] Paraphrases of part of James i, 17 ("Every good gift and every perfect gift is from above, and cometh down from the Father of lights") were often and variously incorporated into formal prayers. For example, one occurs in *"Certaine prayers, taken oute of the seruice dayly, vsed in the queenes house."* These were occasional prayers issued in Elizabeth's reign and appended to *The Prayer-Book of Queen Elizabeth, 1559* (London [1890?]), 152. The most familiar version today occurs in the Prayer for the Clergy in the Book of Common Prayer.

[18] Both canticles may now be used at Evening Prayer according to the Book of Common Prayer. Although Hughes does not recognize the connection with the *Magnificat*, he does cite (p. 350) Job xxxviii, 7, as well as the Biblical source for the *Gloria in*

excelsis as contributory to Milton's *Gloria.* In Job one finds merely that the sons of God shouted for joy at the time of the creation.

[19] For accounts of the ceremony see especially Karl Young, *The Drama of the Medieval Church* (Oxford, 1933), I, 102-104, and E. K. Chambers, *The Mediaeval Stage* (Oxford, 1903), II, 4.

[20] The Form of Consecration of a Church or Chapel is now included with the Ordinal and published in The Book of Common Prayer of the Episcopal Church of the United States. See Massey H. Shepherd, Jr., *The Oxford American Prayer Book Commentary* (New York, 1950), 563-68, for a succinct historical account of the Form.

[21] A similar hymn is sung by the angels following God's pronouncement against Sin and Death when they claim the world. God says they are scavengers; the angels echo Revelation xv, 3, singing "Halleluiah to Him who shall bring new Heaven and new Earth."

[22] A note to this passage in the Index to the *Columbia Milton* (II, 1538) cites this collect in the Prayer Book as source.

[23] Anglican use allows at the beginning of the Eucharist the *Confiteor* in exact literal translation or in a somewhat shortened from, the priest making his confession as well as the acolytes. I quote the shortened form as illustrative: "I confess to Almighty God, the Father, the Son, and the Holy Ghost, before the whole company of Heaven and to thee Father [the priest] that I have sinned exceedingly in thought, word, and deed by my fault, by my own fault, by my own most grievous fault. Wherefore I beg Almighty God to have mercy upon me, and thee, Father, to pray for me to the Lord our God."

[24] *Works*, XVI, 207.

[25] Malcolm Mackenzie Ross, *Poetry & Dogma: The Transfiguration of Eucharistic Symbols in Seventeenth Century English Poetry* (New Brunswick, N.J., 1954), 224.

[26] The pertinent passage in the Apostles' Creed reads: "He ascended into heaven, And sitteth on the right hand of God the Father Almighty: From thence he shall come to judge the quick and the dead." Milton prefers the words added in the Nicene: "*with glory* to judge *both* the quick and the dead." Hughes (n.p. 464) says that "quick and dead" comes from the Apostles' Creed, not recognizing the unmistakable echo from the Nicene. Although Milton says he cannot trust his creed to any church (*Works*, XV, 7) and that "We can want no Creed, so long as we want not the Scriptures" (*Works*, III, Part I, 353), he writes with approval and affection of the Apostles' Creed (*Works*, XIV,

357) when he finds it to support his belief that the Son is inferior to the Father.

3. PARADISE REGAINED

[1] It should be noted that *Paradise Regained* sings the recovery of lost Paradise through one perfect man's firm obedience; it does not sing the restoration of the loss. Through disobedience it was lost; through obedience it is found. To disobey was to act; to obey was to stand. Perfect obedience, not an overt action in itself, assured the final and necessary action—the Passion which earlier was beyond the poet's years to write and which now, guaranteed and made certain, need not be written.

[2] It should be noted that, as in *Paradise Lost,* the poet's invocation is a prayer to the Spirit of God, a divine impulse given from above, to inspire his "prompted Song, else mute." It is of course a ritual, but lacking in the specific petitions one finds in *Paradise Lost* to make it immediately suggest the preacher's prayer before his sermon.

[3] The *Gloria in excelsis* is a patchwork, wonderfully fused, from Luke ii, 14; Psalms cxviii, 26; Luke xix, 38; the *Te Deum;* the *Kyrie;* the *Agnus Dei;* Philippians ii, 11; Acts ii, 36; and 1 Corinthians viii, 6. See Shepherd, *Prayer Book Commentary,* 84, for analysis.

[4] See Barbara Lewalski, *Milton's Brief Epic: The Genre, Meaning, and Art of Paradise Regained* (Providence, R. I., 1966), 314. Mrs. Lewalski observes throughout her work the priestly office of the Son in *Paradise Regained.* At this point especially she notices that the banquet scene "symbolizes the church's communion which celebrates Christ's priestly sacrifice and which prefigures the 'marriage of the Lamb.' "

[5] Whatever reservations Milton may have had regarding the equality and co-eternity of the persons of the Godhead, they do not affect the characterization of the Son in *Paradise Regained.* In fact, the poem is concerned to prove that He is "Very God of Very God."

4. SAMSON AGONISTES

[1] William Riley Parker, *Milton's Debt to Greek Tragedy in "Samson Agonistes"* (Hamden, Conn., 1963), 238. Parker makes much of Samson's hardly won faith, indicating that his struggle

for it runs throughout the testings. I maintain, rather, that the tests follow the achievement of faith as expressed in the confessions, and that the episodes with Dalila, Harapha, and the Officer strengthen him against his sin. They serve the instructional part of the divine services—the lessons and homilies.

[2] See *Liturgies and Occasional forms of Prayer set Forth in the Reign of Queen Elizabeth*. Parker Society, XXX, 265. The Confession in the Communion Service begins following the address to "Almighty God, Father of our Lord Jesus Christ . . . we acknowledge and bewail our manifold sins. . . ." In *The Prayer Book of Queen Elizabeth, 1559*, p. 147, among the "Godly Prayers" a general confession begins: "O Almightie God, our heauenly Father, I confesse and knowledge that I am a miserable and wretched sinner. . . ."

[3] See Joseph Frank, "The Unharmonious Vision: Milton as a Baroque Artist," *Comparative Literature Studies*, III (no. 2), 107, who thinks that as Milton's theology becomes dubious, his art becomes finer. He sees nothing but theological doubt in the irony of Samson's death. The triumph of the Champion in death eludes him.

[4] Another piece of ritual should be noted, though a perverted one. This is Dalila's confession, in which she offers excuses:

> With doubtful feet and wavering resolution
> I came, still dreading thy displeasure, *Samson*,
> Which to have merited, without excuse,
> I cannot but acknowledge; yet if tears
> May expiate (though the fact more evil drew
> In the perverse event that I foresaw)
> My penance hath not slack'n'd, though my pardon
> No way assur'd.   (ll. 732-39)

It is to be contrasted with Samson's confession to his father or with Eve's to Adam. Samson observes a little later that "malice, not repentance brought thee hither" (l. 820).

[5] Professor John Huntley has pointed out that Milton echoes the *Nunc dimittis* twice in *Samson Agonistes*, in lines 687-88 and in lines 1755-57, the very last lines of the poem:

> His servants he with new acquist
> Of true experience from this great event
> With peace and consolation hath dismist,
> And calm of mind, all passion spent.

See "A Revaluation of the Chorus in Milton's *Samson Agonistes*," *Modern Philology*, LXIV (Nov., 1966), 132-45.

CONCLUSION

[1] *A Preface to Paradise Lost* (Oxford, 1952), 39. Lewis's discussion of the opening paragraph of *Paradise Lost* is a brilliant explanation of just how the style of the passage, ritualistic in quality, gives "us the sensation *that some great thing is now about to begin*" (p. 40).

INDEX

Milton, John (*continued*):
to Apocrypha and Song of the Three Holy Children, 30-32, 47; Adam's grace, 32-33, 46, 47; use of canticles, 33-34, 35-36, 36-37, 47; Benediction, 37; Satan's use of liturgy, 38; judgment of Adam and Eve's sin as ritual, 38-39; Eve's confession to Adam, 39-40; Lord's Supper, 40-44; Adam's grace before dinner unrecognized, 47; Adam's visions, 60; as morality play, 67-68; *Paradise Regained*, 55, 64, 65; sacrament of Baptism, 49-50; structural function of, 54; use of canticles, 50-51; lament and prayer of Apostles, 51-52; Mary's meditation, 52-53; references and suggestions of liturgy, 52-53; final anthem of angels, 52-54; relation to Nicene Creed, 53-54; similarity to canticle of praise, 54; structural functions of rituals and liturgical sections, 54; *Samson Agonistes*, 65, 68; its liturgical pattern, 55-62; chorus, 57; Samson's confession, 57-58; Samson's contrition, 58-59; chorus' prayer for absolution, 60; Samson's testing, 60-61; Manoa's speech, relation to Burial of the Dead, 61-62; play as sacrament, 62
Milton, John, Sr., musician, 3
Miserere mei, Deus, 10
Myriell, Thomas, *Tristitiae Remedivm*, 3-4

Nicene Creed, 46, 53-54
Nunc dimittis, 4, 48, 61

Oblation, in Prayer Books of Edward VI, 43; in Scottish Prayer Book of 1637, 43
Officer, 60

Parker, William Riley, 56
Paul, St., 56

Pax vobiscum, 2, 11, 65
Penetential Psalms, 10
Peter, St., 2
Prayer Book, Scottish, 4; first of Edward VI, Collect for Burial of the Dead, 12-13
Prayer of Humble Access, 58
Psalm: xxii, for Good Friday, 7; li, 10; lxxiv and cxxvii, 29; xxiv, 35, 36; cxii, 36; xcviii, 37; xcv, *Venite* of Morning Prayer, 37; c, *Jubilate Deo* of Morning Prayer, 37; xxiv, 47; xcviii, *Cantate Domino* of Evening Prayer, 51; cxxiv, 54; xiv and viii, 57; xxxvii and viii, 60; lxxxix, 61
Psychomachia, and Samson's soul-struggle, 56

Raphael, doctrine of accommodation, 44
Ravenscroft, Thomas, compendium of church music, 3; *Whole Book of Psalms*, 4
Revelation, 7, 13, 26; iv, v, xix, 37; xiv, xv, 50; ix, 54; xv, 57; xiv, 61
Ross, Malcolm Mackenzie, 44-45

Sandys, George, Psalm paraphrases, 4
Satan, 49
Second Shepherds' Play, 16
Service of Burial of the Dead, 62
Shakespeare, William, 59
Spenser, Edmund, 2, 61; *Faerie Queene*, Books I and II, 17; Sapience, 21
Sternhold and Hopkins, 4
Suetonius, 23
Summers, Joseph H., 31

Taylor, Jeremy, compiler of liturgies, 4
Te Deum, 4
Triton, 2

Venite, 4
Virgil, 2, 15

83

CPSIA information can be obtained at www.ICGtesting.com
Printed in the USA
BVOW05s1429090714

358655BV00001B/10/P